# Program Management Redefined

## Techniques to Improve

## Organizational Agility

James F. Carilli, Ph.D., PfMP, PgMP, PMP

Aurora Corialis Publishing

Pittsburgh, PA

Program Management Redefined: Techniques to Improve Organizational Agility

Paperback ISBN: 978-1-958481-02-8
EBook ISBN: 978-1-958481-03-5
Printed in the United States of America

Cover by Karen Captline, BetterBe Creative
Edited by Greg Leatherman

# Praise for *Program Management Redefined*

"An excellent and unique approach to program management by Dr. Carilli. I'm sure this work will become a benchmark in the industry."

– Mike Sutton, PMP, Lead Project Manager, EPA Enterprise Content Management System (Ret.)

"Jim shares his wealth of knowledge in a concise and easy to follow book that provides specific techniques to improve organizational agility for programs. The framework he presents is not only practical but immediately applicable for those in the profession to leverage today. With such limited agile guidance for programs, it is refreshing to see a contemporary approach to program management."

– Mike Harkins, Agile Transformation Coach with certifications from Scrum.org, Scrum Alliance, and SAFe | Founder of The Harkins Leadership Group

"Based on more than 30 years of experience, Dr. Carilli provides a comprehensive guide to program management designed to avoid the pitfalls of traditional practices. A good read filled with useful insights."

– Dr. W. Tad Foster, Professor Emeritus, former Dean of the College of Technology, Indiana State University

"The interrelationships among product, project, program, and portfolio management are often misunderstood. Although these disciplines are often discussed independently, they must work seamlessly together to propel forward a series of successful deliverables. Dr. Carilli, leveraging his years of experience, has done exactly that, provided techniques to successfully traverse and navigate the interrelationships among the disciplines to provide positive organizational outcomes. This book provides clear guidance on the building blocks and bridges the dependency gaps with clear definitions and examples."

– Sahil Saini, Director FP&A, Princess Cruises

# Acknowledgements

My journey through the creation of this book would not have been possible without the support of many people. I would like to extend my sincere gratitude to those who served as trusted advisors and technical editors for this book: Huy Cat, Mike Harkins, Dr. W. Tad Foster, and Mike Sutton. I've learned a great deal from my association with all of you over the years. Thank you so much for sharing your time, experience, knowledge, and expertise. The book is so much better as a result of your contributions.

Heartfelt thanks to my wife, best friend, and number one cheerleader, Debi Donaldson. Your love, patience, and constant encouragement helped me to remain focused throughout this book. Words cannot express my true appreciation for all you've done. I owe you a great debt of gratitude (and probably a vacation). Sincere thanks to my father, Albert J. Carilli, whose pursuit of lifelong learning served as an inspiration and strong influence in this quest.

Many thanks to Cori Wamsley of Aurora Corialis Publishing for your mentoring, training, consulting, coaching and overall guidance in the development and publishing of this book. You helped me achieve a life-long goal and I am truly grateful for your help. To Karen Captline of BetterBeCreative, thank you for sharing your talented hand and creativity in creating the book cover, logo, web design, and overall branding for Program Agility LLC and ProgramAgility.com. To my editor, Greg Leatherman, I remain in awe of your command of the language and gift of composition. I am truly grateful for your contributions, multiple edits, and rewrites. You made this a better product.

I'd like to thank and recognize the authors who wrote the books, articles, conference papers, and other publications I referenced throughout this book. I am so appreciative of your contributions to the profession.

Finally, I'd like to thank my family, friends, and professional colleagues who provided balance, insights, and encouragement along the way.

# Table of Contents

# List of Figures

# Preface

Many new management practices emerged over the past few years focused on improving organizational agility at the delivery team level. While initially created for manufacturing and more recently applied to software development, the benefits of "agile" practices and supporting methods have been applied throughout many business areas and have had a direct and tangible impact on many aspects of organizational success. Numerous case studies demonstrate the value of agile practices. The benefits include increased productivity, shorter cycle times, reduced risk, improved strategic alignment, simplified processes, lower costs, and greater customer satisfaction.

Despite all these benefits, there is limited literature providing guidance on how to increase agility for program management practices. The time has come to redefine the program management discipline to focus on improving organizational agility at the program level.

Program Management Redefined

After more than three decades of providing project, program, and portfolio management support to many organizations, I wrote this book to give back to the profession that has served me so well. I've been afforded many opportunities to support the profession by volunteering for several Global standards efforts as a Vice-Chair, Committee Member, Contributing Author, and Subject Matter Expert Reviewer, presenting research and perspectives at academic and professional conferences, serving as a guest lecturer for MBA students, mentoring those starting their careers in project and program management, and training and coordinating training for scores of professionals seeking industry certifications.

Through these experiences, I have seen first-hand the evolution of organizational agility and the direct and tangible benefits provided by today's practices to those organizations that employ them. The intent of this book is to share those insights in the hope of helping others in program management and associated disciplines, so you may reap the benefits agile practices provide in your area of focus and expertise.

For over forty years, the elements of agility have been studied and documented and we are now seeing organizations embrace these practices at both the delivery team level and more recently at the program level. In 1979, the Center for Organizational Effectiveness at USC Marshall School of Business was established and reviewed over 500 organizations. Soon after, they developed models to measure organizational agility. The outcomes of this research are documented on their website, as well as in *Assessing Organization Agility: Creating Diagnostic Profiles to Guide Transformation* (Worley, Williams & Lawler, 2014) and in Appendix C of this book.

In his 1987 #1 best-selling book *Thriving on Chaos,* Tom Peters described subject areas that very closely match today's Agile guidance (customer responsiveness, fast-paced innovation, empowering people, learning to love change, and revamping processes to support these goals). Finally, in 1991, the term "Agile Manufacturing" was coined at the Iacocca Institute at Lehigh University.

Over twenty years ago, the Agile Alliance was formed by a "group of independent thinkers about software development." In the same year, these seventeen signatories authored *Agile Manifesto for Software Development* (2001). More recently, the Project Management Institute ® published the *Agile Practice Guide*

(2017). That guide recognizes a change in the role of the Project Manager on Agile projects. With the introduction of Agile methods, in some organizations, some tasks traditionally performed at the delivery team level by Project Managers shift to the Program Management team.

Agile@Scale methods have emerged over the past two decades. Disciplined Agile® Delivery, Dynamic Systems Delivery Method [DSDM], Large Scale Scrum [LeSS], Scaled Agile Framework® [SAFe], Nexus Framework, Recipes for Agile Governance in the Enterprise™ [RAGE], Scrum of Scrums [SoS], Scaling Agile @ Spotify [Spotify Model], and others are having an impact at both the project and program level (and some at the portfolio level). While many of the methods and frameworks focus on software delivery, some need to provide additional guidance for the supporting infrastructure and business practices.

In the past two decades, technological innovations have changed the way businesses identify, define, design, develop, test, deliver, support, and market products and services. 3D printing, 5G networks, artificial intelligence, augmented reality, automation, blockchain, business intelligence, cloud computing, conversational chatbots, digitization, internet of things (IoT), low/no code solutions, quantum computing, touchscreen and infinity displays, social media, virtual reality, virtual assistants, and a variety of other innovations have not only changed how we work but have changed what and how we deliver.

Other notable management practices are emerging and becoming part of how we do work. Systems thinking is helping us analyze not only the system, but how its components interrelate and affect other constituent parts over time. Design thinking is changing our approach to problem-solving and helping organizations improve products and services. It helps by prioritizing and focusing on customer needs, prototyping, and testing potential solutions. Finally, DevOps, the close collaboration of development and operations teams, has moved far beyond breaking down the long-standing communications barriers (silos) between these teams. DevOps today is highlighted by a continual flow of releases inextricably linking the two formerly separate entities. DevOps brings with it changes relative to culture, structure, practices, processes, and tools. By doing so, collaboration, speed, scalability, and reliability of the outcomes are positively impacted.

So much has changed in the past two decades and yet the current program management standards and literature contain too little guidance on how to address, adopt, and apply these techniques. This book provides a "redefined" framework for program management based on the desire to increase organizational agility, and address the practices outlined above while considering the current and proposed functions performed at the program level.

In my 30+ years of helping global organizations with complex projects and programs, I have been very fortunate to have opportunities, mentors, and experiences that helped shape the content of this book. With that said, I did not solely reference my experience in writing this book. I shared the manuscript with my network from the business and academic communities and reviewed several case studies, recently published books, articles, journal papers, conference proceedings, videos, and other media, prior to publishing. I hope you find the ideas contained within helpful, and I welcome your feedback so we may engage in a dialogue about your thoughts and ideas and learn from our collective experiences.

# Introduction

# Introduction

Whether a business struggles or thrives depends on its ability to recognize and respond to market changes. There are too many case studies about organizations with a significant market advantage that failed to recognize changes in their customer's current or future needs and did not realign their strategy to meet those changes, resulting in loss of market position – in some cases leading to insolvency. Other organizations were presented with great opportunities and failed to deliver against those objectives – resulting in negative changes in their market position and/or the erosion of customer confidence.

In the public company case study of Blockbuster, we see a strategy failure. What worked well in the past did not position them well for the future. Blockbuster led the home movie rental market with over 9,100 brick-and-mortar storefronts in 2004 (Zax, 2011). When rival competitors (Netflix and Hulu) entered the market,

Blockbuster doubled down on video game sales instead of focusing on the competition for their core offering, movie rentals. At one point, Blockbuster passed up the opportunity to acquire Netflix "for a mere $50 million" (Davis and Higgins, 2013, pp 1). Despite this opportunity, the bigger picture was that they truly failed to sense and respond to customer changing needs with the advent of the internet streaming and expansion of on-demand capabilities through "cable" television providers (including satellite, fiber optic, etc.).

Jeffery Stegenga, Blockbuster Chief Restructuring Officer, described Blockbuster's challenges stemming from five key events (Davis & Higgins, 2013, pp 7.): (1) increased competition in the media entertainment industry; (2) technological advances that changed the landscape of the industry; (3) changing consumer preferences; (4) the rapid growth of disruptive new competitors; and (5) the general economic environment. Netflix, Hulu, Amazon Prime, and premium "cable" channels (HBO, Showtime, Cinemax, others) provided streaming and on-demand offerings that eroded the remaining market share from Blockbuster. In 2010, Blockbuster closed operations. In the end, it was Blockbuster's failure to recognize a changing market and sense and respond to their customers' needs that paved their way into bankruptcy.

Just as concerning as not following the right strategy is not being able to successfully deliver on that strategy. On March 23, 2010, the Affordable Care Act (ACA) became law. The law required nearly all Americans to obtain health insurance either through their employer or a government provided healthcare marketplace. At the center of this was a proposed website (Healthcare.gov) where consumers could shop for health plans. ACA's rushed implementation of the HealthCare.gov website became one of the most highly publicized failures in the history of government software development. When the website was opened for enrollment, many potential users experienced problems accessing the site, and those who could connect found the user experience so challenging they ultimately weren't able to purchase healthcare from the site.

The Centers for Medicare and Medicaid Services (CMS) within the U.S. Department of Health and Human Services (HHS) was charged with ensuring website functionality. Dr. Gwanhoo Lee and Justin Brumer's 2017 case study stated, "CMS was confronted with a barrage of political and programmatic issues from the project inception that included (p. 70):

- Project complexity,
- Uncertainty,
- Compressed timeframe high-risk contracts, and
- Lack of senior leadership."

They concluded that despite the "daunting challenge," if project and program management *fundamentals* were in place and adhered to, these disciplines "would have prevented the devastating failure (p. 74)."

After struggling in 2013, in 2014 a new systems integrator was brought in, and CMS addressed many of their management shortcomings. The website was successfully relaunched in late-2014 for the 2015 benefit period. The HHS Office of the Inspector General's 2016 report found the "key factors that contributed to recovery of the website included adopting a 'badgeless' culture for the project, wherein all CMS staff and contractors worked together as a team, and a practice of 'ruthless prioritization' that aligned work efforts with the most important and [setting] achievable goals."

The original systems integrator lost both the confidence of this customer and had to carry the burden of those who remember their involvement as a part of their resume. A great opportunity was missed, not only through their own doing, but also through their inability to collaborate well with the customer.

# Program Management Redefined

# A Call to Action

The case studies presented above underscore the importance of organizational agility and discipline in portfolio, program, project, and product management practices. At first glance one may think that agility and discipline are diametrically opposed considerations. Agility indeed requires management support to foster an organizational culture that is customer focused, responsive, innovative, and empowers team members. At the same time, to meet these goals, discipline in the form of systems, policies, processes, and practices needs to be in place, albeit with a new approach.

The case studies presented (and many more) plus the considerations discussed in the Preface of this book stand as a call to action to redefine Program Management and to present principles, themes, and techniques that improve organizational agility, and a framework with associated practices to meet the needs of today. The Program Delivery Framework presented in Part III provides new considerations for increasing organizational agility, while factoring in emerging Program Management practices.

## Redefined Defined

Many factors went into selecting the appropriate title for this book. The base definition of program management is found in standards. This book uses those standards as the foundation for "redefining" program management. The Standard for Program Management (PMI, 2017) states its objective is to describe *"what constitutes good practice on most programs most of the time* (p. 143)." The 2023 version (5th Edition) of the standard hasn't yet been publicly released, but in reviewing the document during the *Draft Comment Period (DCP)* it appears that this objective will remain.

*Program Management Redefined: Techniques to Improve Organizational Agility,* presents forward leaning, yet immediately usable and pragmatic practices for program management. The methods, practices, and techniques described within may have not crossed the chasm into "most programs most of the time," yet. But where these practices are deployed, the benefits achieved are accelerating that momentum. Specific areas of *redefinition* in this book include:

- **An agility-inspired framework:** The Program Delivery Framework stands as a new, simplified, and focused model for program management that emphasizes delivery support versus management oversight as the name implies. The framework harmonizes best practices, consolidates redundant practices, removes legacy project practices from the program model and eliminates outdated practices.

- **Streamlined guidance and updated practices:** The Core Practice Areas of Governance, Strategic Alignment, and Delivery Support, as well as their associated guiding principles, promote a culture that leverages Lean/Agile methods, processes, and practices.

- **Organizational change management focus:** The probability of success is greatly influenced by addressing the human side of change. Understanding the type of change, and the correct methods to apply, yields greater user acceptance resulting in more consistent program outcomes.

- **New management and decision-support tools:** Several new models are presented (e.g., 5P Decision Support Matrix, MUSIC Stakeholder Map, RICE Matrix, etc.).

- **Organizational agility techniques:** Many themes are introduced to guide program practices. Dozens of techniques for organizational agility are provided within each program management practice based on the themes.
- **Full program delivery lifecycle activities:** Practical and immediately usable methods to address each practice area based on real world successes.
- **A full suite of measures and metrics:** Including an organizational agility assessment and measures of success from which to plan and evaluate progress and describe outcomes.

While some practices may be shared within the current standard, they are presented here with a focus on improving organizational agility.

## The Case for Program Management

Program management provides organizational value by coordinating the efforts of multiple teams to achieve strategic goals. It's more than an overhead function or collection of similar projects and changes managed under the same umbrella. "Effective program management ensures people and teams are focused and collaborating across departments who are working together to achieve a shared strategic vision" (Roach, 2023). Program managers meet the organization's strategic objectives by providing governance, strategic alignment, and delivery support. Program management can bring a several business benefits, including (Brown, 2022; Harrin, 2022; Hatfield 2016; Roach, 2023):

- **Improved alignment and coordination:** Program management can help align the goals and objectives of individual change activities (process changes, new and enhanced products, projects, organizational change activities, services, solutions, other activities, or desired results) with the overall business strategy, improving coordination and reducing duplication of effort.

- **Enhanced risk management:** By overseeing multiple change activities, program managers can identify, manage, and mitigate cross-team risks more efficiently, reducing the impact of potential issues.

- **Increased efficiency:** Program management can help streamline processes, reduce waste, and increase efficiency through standardization of processes and the coordinated allocation of resources to ensure the effective use of finances.

- **Enhanced visibility:** Program management provides a higher-level view of the change activities under its purview than managing them separately. Senior leadership decisions can be supported through the use of summarized information and relevant metrics created by program teams.

- **Improved stakeholder management:** Program management can be used to reduce the number of contacts a stakeholder needs to consult to gather information. Program teams may also develop information repositories for stakeholders (e.g., Program Intranet site, etc.) for self-service access to role-based information, improving communications and ensuring that their needs and concerns are effectively addressed.

- **Increased agility:** Program management enables organizations to respond faster to changes in the business environment by supporting the ability to adjust, prioritize, and make decisions more effectively as priorities shift, even across the portfolio or organization.

- **Expanded team collaboration:** Cross-team internal and external interdependencies can be visualized, assessed, and addressed to aid in meeting both committed and expected customer requirements.
- **Improved Return on Investment (ROI):** By ensuring that resources are used effectively (and shared if possible), reducing waste, and improving processes, program management can help improve the return on investment for a group of aligned change activities.

There are a few cases noted below where establishing a program management team may not be the right solution. In these cases, the portfolio team may directly provide support delivery teams without a formal program management structure. These cases may include:

- The number of delivery teams is relatively small (i.e., fewer than three) and there is little complexity.

- The need to limit the exposure of a change activity to fewer people due to intellectual property rights, security, confidentiality reasons, or based on management discretion.
- The change activities for a delivery team are truly independent and would not realize the benefits provided by a program.

Overall, program management can help organizations achieve business objectives more effectively and efficiently. By improving strategic alignment, supporting cross-team collaboration and coordination, optimizing resource utilization, managing risks, streamlining stakeholder engagement, and providing many other benefits, program management is essential to organizational success.

## Intended Audience

This book was primarily written for those currently serving in program management roles or those who aspire to enter the profession. For both audiences, the content is intended to provide a new way of thinking about programs through the lenses of organizational agility and simplified, yet comprehensive, practice areas and guiding principles. The Program Delivery Framework provides a structure for solutions through the integration of practices and interactions with key stakeholders.

Portfolio Managers, Program Sponsors, Program Steering Committee members, and Senior Business and IT leadership may benefit from this book to gain knowledge regarding:

- Assessing the business case for the investment in program management and promoting the benefits of program management.
- Identifying opportunities to deploy program management teams to support the delivery of strategic business objectives.
- Providing support and guidance to program management teams.
- Evaluating potential candidates for upcoming program management opportunities or when assigning additional responsibilities.
- Understanding the program roles and competencies to offer learning and development opportunities to those who aspire to program management roles.

Program Management Redefined

# Part I: Program Management in Context

# Part I:

# Program Management in

# Context

No two programs are alike. Each has its own purpose, goals, and objectives. Even the term used to describe programs themselves often differs. Numerous definitions of program management can be found in standards, books, conference papers, academic and trade journals and other print and on-line publications. Most consider program management as primarily an oversight function and neglect to recognize the support function provided to aid delivery teams. This book

> **Program Management**
> A governance and delivery support function that aligns organizational strategies with change and operational activities to provide benefits to stakeholders.

redefines Program Management as a governance and delivery support function that aligns organizational strategies with change and operational activities to provide benefits to stakeholders.

Programs consist of change activities that share a common impact area or organizational goal. These change activities can take various forms, such as process changes, new and improved products, projects, organizational changes, services, solutions, or other activities that align with the specific needs of the organization. By organizing these change activities as a program, organizations can achieve greater coordination, collaboration, consistency, transparency, strategic alignment, and visibility to stakeholders who are performing or affected by these changes. This approach provides more benefits than managing these activities separately.

# Chapter 1:
# Relationship Among Teams

Following the development of the overall organizational strategy, there are generally four entities involved in the identification, authorization, definition, coordination, delivery, and support of change activities in organizations. These are organized as Portfolio, Program, Delivery and Operations teams. The relationships among these teams vary based on the organizational needs. Figure 1 provides two conceptual views commonly applied to the relationships between these entities. Note that Figure 1 shows working relationships and team alignments. This is not intended to suggest reporting relationships like those found in organization charts.

| Traditional | "Redefined" |
|---|---|
| Portfolio<br>Program<br>Delivery<br>Operations | Portfolio<br>Program<br>Delivery  Operations |

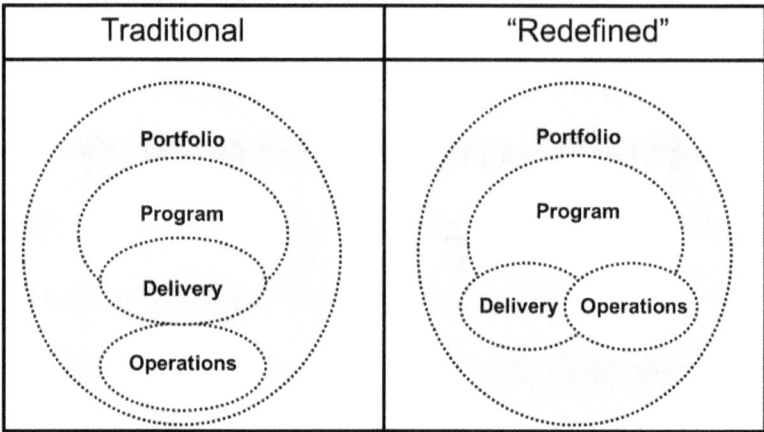

*Figure 1*. Programs provide a governance, alignment, and delivery support function by aligning the strategy defined at the portfolio level with the change activities performed by the delivery and operations teams.

In many organizations, the portfolio function provides governance primarily for programs and operations teams. The programs then support multiple delivery teams. As the delivery teams complete their work, they then transition the completed work to operations teams.

In the "redefined" model, the portfolio team continues to govern the program and operations teams. However, in this model, the program teams also support both the delivery and operations functions as change activities are constantly deployed. For the changes to be effectively supported and managed, the alignment and smooth transition of the change activities from the delivery to the operations teams, along with support from the program team, are crucial. This connection between the delivery and operations teams is referred to as "DevOps."

DevOps grew out of software development activities, however, today, its core concepts are widely used for change activities performed by both business and IT delivery teams on both software and "non-software" changes. As an example, in the past most software projects were performed using the Waterfall method. With this sequential method, software (and/or hardware, et Al.) teams would spend months developing large amounts of new code for new products or for enhancements to existing applications. Often the operations teams would be left out of the planning, design, development, and testing process and were primarily (or solely) engaged at the end when the changes were ready for production. These "big bang" deployment efforts were, in some cases, so significant that it would take literally months to integrate the changes into the existing code base in production (managed by operations teams). By not involving the operations teams (and many other change support areas) early in the process, major problems and significant delays were encountered. To mitigate these problems, agile software development methods were employed along with the concept of DevOps. DevOps was initially started to simply bridge the communications gap between delivery and operations teams. Today, DevOps includes many activities to create a partnership between delivery and operations teams to support the continuous delivery of new change activities. DevOps will be discussed in detail later in this book (Chapter 20).

In the *current* model, the operations teams are shown without a connection to the program team. This too was problematic considering programs provide support to multiple delivery teams, it becomes important to align these change activities with those who will eventually support them. Adding in the DevOps culture, it is imperative for

> **Change Activities**
> May include process changes, new and enhanced products, projects, organizational change activities, services, solutions, other activities, or desired results associated with that program based on the specific needs of the performing organization.

Programs to align with both delivery and operations teams. The "redefined" model depicts a direct relationship. While the portfolio team will still provide support to operations teams, it is paramount for program (and delivery) team(s) to collaborate with operations considering the number of potential changes and cross coordination of efforts among multiple delivery and operations teams.

The entities shown in Figure 1 interact based on the needs of the sponsoring organization. The dotted lines encompassing each function indicate the flow of communications and collaboration between and amongst the teams. The portfolio team also has a dotted line indicating their interactions with a wide variety of stakeholders.

Figure 2 (below) provides additional detail on the redefined arrangement and alignment of associated functions. Portfolio 1 is comprised of two program teams supporting five and seven delivery teams, respectively. In this arrangement, the portfolio team also has oversight for two operational support teams. The portfolio manager may have chosen to charter the two program teams separately because their initiatives are logically separate but internally aligned for that portfolio.

For example, the programs may be related to separate business process change initiatives where the stakeholders and delivery teams are logically separate from each other (e.g., Financial, Supply Chain, Customer Relationship Management, etc.) but each program is aligned with a single or group of strategic goals associated with that sponsoring portfolio (or product line).

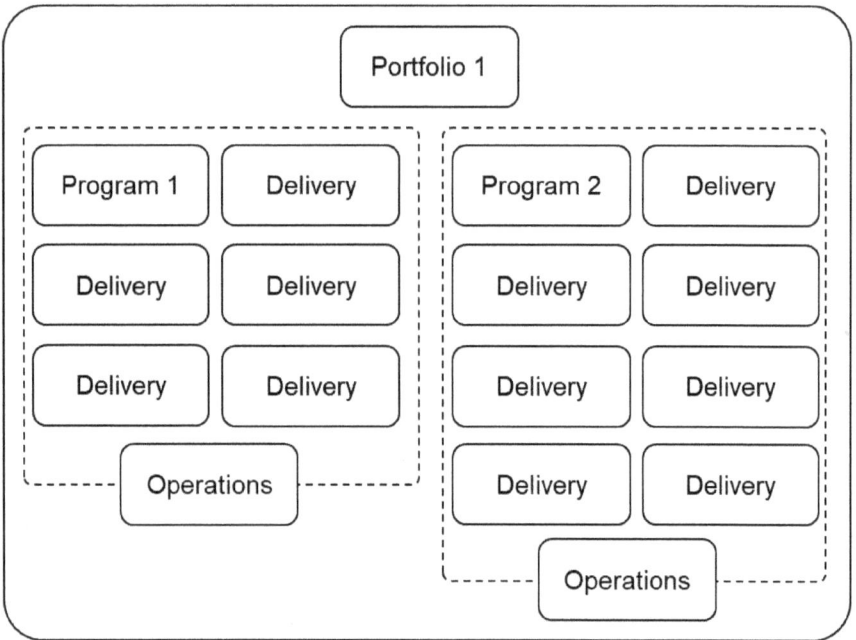

Portfolio 1

| Program 1 | Delivery | Program 2 | Delivery |
| Delivery | Delivery | Delivery | Delivery |
| Delivery | Delivery | Delivery | Delivery |
| Operations | | Delivery | Delivery |
| | | Operations | |

*Figure 2.* Portfolio, Program, Delivery, and Operations Teams relationships may vary based on the nature of the work performed or the needs of the sponsoring organization.

The number of delivery teams may vary based on the work effort required to achieve the goals of the program. Delivery teams for software applications may include multiple software development teams, infrastructure, security, network, testing and delivery support teams (e.g., Organizational Change Management, Stakeholder Communications, etc.) as appropriate. The operations teams are depicted with a partial relationship to the program and the portfolio.

Operations teams generally have two responsibilities: 1) support and maintain their respective operational function (often managed separately [from programs] and in collaboration with the portfolio team) and 2) prepare for and integrate changes into the operational baseline provided by external organizations (e.g., changes delivered by Program Delivery teams; changes directly from delivery teams; maintenance activities [e.g., software patches, etc.] and others).

Another scenario, not shown in the diagram, could be a portfolio directly managing a single team or a group of delivery teams without the presence of a program function, for reasons explained earlier. Although the core functions of each area are generally similar, the dotted lines in the diagram illustrate the variability in how these functions are performed and by which entity, depending on the organizational structure. Further variations of the organizational arrangements depicted above could include a portfolio leading a single or group of sub-portfolios or a program providing support for a single or group of subordinate programs. To better comprehend these relationships, it is essential to understand the core functions of each entity and identify areas where there may be variability.

# Chapter 2:
# Core Team Functions

Each of the organizational entities (i.e., Portfolio, Program, Delivery, and Operations teams) employ common practices intended to deliver organizational benefits. Due to myriad organizational design arrangements, it is more important to understand the functions being performed than the names associated with the organizational entities (Portfolio, Program, etc.). This chapter introduces the core functions of the four teams, while Chapter 3 will expand upon the information below with a detailed example showing these functions in action through the various roles that support these functions.

Since more teams are embracing Agile methods, in some organizations, there is a shift of some of the tasks traditionally performed by Project Managers (at the delivery team level) to the program level. As Agile methods have emerged, in some cases, Project Managers have been replaced with Scrum Masters. A new hybrid Scrum Master/Project Manager role may have been established to accommodate the responsibilities of both roles; in others, the program team has taken on the responsibilities not performed at the delivery team level.

An example of a task traditionally performed by a Project Manager and not generally performed by a Scrum Master is the management of a budget. In this example a Project Manager is not assigned, and a Scrum Master is assigned to support the work and facilitate Scrum ceremonies. Without a Project Manager to manage the budget, the Scrum Master may either be requested to take on this added responsibility, in a hybrid role, or the program team may be requested to take on this task. In either case, the task to manage the budget is still performed, but in this case it is done at the program level versus the delivery team level.

Please note that the sections that follow are provided for a contextual understanding regarding their relationship to the program team functions. They are not intended as an exhaustive listing of all aspects for each functional area. Also, there are many variables in organizations, therefore, the information below may be considered as a guideline for common functions within each functional area.

## Portfolio Management Core Functions

The Portfolio Management function is critical to governing the alignment with and attainment of organizational strategies. The portfolio team performs several functions to identify, prioritize, organize, and allocate resources (e.g., financial, facilities, human, material, technology, etc.) and manage change activities by "investing" in initiatives that align with and provide value to the overall organizational

> **Portfolio Management**
> an organizational function that prioritizes and allocates resources (e.g., financial, facilities, human, material, technology, etc.) to change activities by "investing" in initiatives that align with organizational strategies.

strategy. As discussed earlier, these change activities may be organized as programs, delivery teams directly leading change activities (comprised of projects, products, change activities, or other supporting functions), and/or operations teams. The scope of the work authorized by portfolio team is variable, as the strategy of the organization requires.

The functions described below may also vary based on the capabilities of the teams and needs of the organization.

Considering rapidly changing market conditions, the portfolio team must put in place strategies and methods that prepare the organization to sense and respond and keep pace with the new and emerging customer requirements and new customer channels. As discussed in the introduction, the ability to sense and respond to changes can mean the difference between an organization that will thrive or one that will be overtaken by its competitors.

To meet these requirements, the organization must be structured with dynamic flexibility, with both proactive and responsive methods, to quickly assess, innovate, and expand capacity to mobilize their resources around these strategic opportunities as they emerge. The outcomes of a successful portfolio management team are dependent upon how well they perform their key functions. These include (Cottmeyer, 2011):

- Managing comprehensive life-cycle plans (using a data-informed and risk managed processes that consider inherent uncertainty in change activities);

- Establishing a stable and predictable organizational capacity;
- Obtaining fast feedback (from internal, external, and potential future stakeholders) to rapidly mitigate risk and manage stakeholder expectations;
- Flexible resource models and rapid innovation to ease of strategic direction of changes and take advantage of opportunities; and
- Transparency of process and progress (to understand capacity and predict value), and respect for people.

To meet these goals, the portfolio team performs several key functions. The functions include, but are not limited to, (Goncalves, 2020; PMI, 2017):

- Aligning resources with strategic objectives,
- Selecting and authorizing value-added investments,
- Compiling information to support management decision-making,
- Overseeing the portfolio life cycle,
- Facilitating continuous strategic planning,
- Planning organizational capacity,

- Assessing business risks and developing mitigation plans,
- Prioritizing initiatives by business value,
- Continually implementing process improvements,
- Actively engaging key stakeholders.

Additional interactions between the portfolio and program teams are detailed in Part IV and Part V of this book.

## Program Management Core Functions

The program management team collaborates with the portfolio team to support the organization's objectives. As organizational strategies are established, and programs are authorized, the program teams initiate activities to identify and allocate resources to deliver the work to meet the intended business benefits. Programs are authorized and

> **Program Management**
> The primary purpose of a program is to maximize the value delivered (in terms of organizational and customer benefits) by effectively allocating resources.

governed by the portfolio management function to deliver

benefits to support the organization's strategies. A program may be established in a few scenarios; these events may include when the portfolio team:

- Considers how to structure a new group of change activities that is being proposed. They may choose to structure these as a program from the onset.
- Has a group of existing individual change activities that they would like to manage as a single program to receive the benefits of that grouping.
- One or more existing programs are running, and the portfolio team deems it to be more beneficial to consolidate and manage as a single program.
- Individual change activities from multiple programs are consolidated into a separate program considering the nature of the work and benefits they would realize by being grouped differently.

Certainly, there are several potential scenarios, however, this illustrates that programs are not always or only chartered for a group of *new* change activities.

# Program Management Redefined

The primary purpose of a program is to maximize the value delivered (in terms of organizational and customer benefits) by effectively allocating resources across the program and delivery functions. By grouping change activities into programs many benefits are achieved through the functions provided. These functions include:

- Facilitating the achievement of organizational strategies by prioritizing and aligning change activities with organizational goals;
- Providing cross team visibility on the progress of change activities included in the program;
- Ensuring the portfolio "investments" are realizing the intended benefits;
- Coordinating organizational change management activities to minimize impact to stakeholders and providing effective communications and stakeholder collaboration to aid in deliveries;
- Enhancing quality and lower rework complexity through design thinking, prototyping, process improvement, and DevOps practices;

- Supporting self-organized/self-managed teams through cross team collaboration and developing processes and guardrails between the functions;
- Providing opportunities for learning and development of core skills, delivery processes, and organizational goals through formal and informal training;
- Effectively managing resources and aligning costs across multiple change activities;
- Managing program uncertainty through risk and issue management to minimize or mitigate potential impacts;
- Providing comprehensive and transparent views through real-time dashboards of program activities for team and management visibility;
- Aligning priorities and managing interdependencies between and among change and operations activities to facilitate a smooth transition; and
- Maintaining common processes and practices by simplifying processes through Kaizen and/or continuous improvement events to reduce complexity and redundant costs.

Parts III and IV of this book will cover the areas described above in more detail.

## Delivery Teams Core Functions

Delivery teams are cross functional, self-managed, and semi-autonomous in that they lead and contribute to the organizational objectives by performing work in their respective areas of expertise on a single or group of a change activities. Unlike the portfolio and program teams, delivery teams are those who perform the work to complete the specified change activity. Teams are self-managed as the members share the responsibilities of planning and performing their work without a formal manager (however, a facilitator may be utilized to help manage the flow of work [e.g., Project Manager, Scrum Master, etc.]). They are semi-autonomous considering they

> ### Delivery Teams
> Are cross functional, self-managed, and semi-autonomous. *Cross functional* in that the team is formed with the appropriate expertise to perform the change activities. *Self-managed* as the members share the responsibilities of planning and performing their work. *Semi-autonomous* because they are directly responsible for the delivery of their assigned change activities.

work independently but often require assistance from other organizations to support the delivery, integration and/or adoption of changes. Delivery support teams may include business functional areas, communications, contracts, finance, human resources (HCM), legal, operations, technology support areas, etc. The first and foremost delivery support organization is the program team using the *redefined* Program Delivery Framework presented in Part III.

Since delivery teams directly manage their work, they may choose to structure their work using a method or a combination of methods that are most advantageous to the type of change required. For example, delivery teams whose change activities are relative to software may choose (Agile) Scrum or another iterative method to perform their work. Another team may choose Waterfall given limited scope and complexity and the tasks are sequential for that change activity. Others may employ a Kanban method, where work is visual and performed in sequence, downstream teams may pull forward work up to their capacity level (limiting work in progress) as the predecessor work is completed. In all cases, but in Kanban specifically, the teams focus on flow and opportunities for improvement.

Based on the method chosen, this may have an impact on the work performed by the program team in support of that delivery team. For example, some delivery teams may not have the expertise in risk management. Therefore, the program and delivery teams will collaborate to determine how best to fill this need. It may be determined that it is best to be performed by the program team, or a resource will be requested (e.g., Project Manager) to perform this responsibility within that delivery team.

Depending upon the method of delivery discussed below, the team may conduct their work differently. This variability makes it difficult to describe specifically which functions are performed by delivery teams, however, as discussed earlier, the functions listed below are common to support delivery, regardless of which team performs them. The delivery teams perform the following functions:

- Aligning their work to the organizational strategy by collaborating with the product owners or program team on prioritization.
- Delivering the work within their allocated scope.
- Managing the budget for the work allocated.

- Maintaining a plan of record and sharing status of change activities included in their scope with key stakeholders (including the program team).
- Directly managing or collaborating with the program team on organizational change management activities to minimize impact to stakeholders.
- Enhancing quality to lower rework and complexity through user experience (UX), design thinking, prototyping, process improvement, and DevOps practices.
- Providing effective communications and stakeholder collaboration to aid in deliveries.
- Supporting opportunities for learning and development of core skills, delivery processes and organizational goals through formal and informal training provided by the delivery team, the program, or another organization.
- Effectively managing resources (e.g., financial, facilities, human, material, technology, etc.) across multiple change activities.
- Managing uncertainty through risk and issue management to minimize or mitigate potential impacts.

While many of the items above are shared with the program team, this is intentional. The delivery teams have or share a significant role in delivering the changes necessary for the organization to meet its objectives.

## Operations Teams Core Functions

Operations teams (aka Operations & Maintenance [O&M]) include the functions, duties, and responsibilities associated with integration and subsequent daily operations and the ongoing support functions within that organization. Responsibilities may include customer service (customer care), emergency break/fix services, routine maintenance, parts replacement, and other activities needed to sustain the organizational/physical assets so that they continue to provide acceptable service and achieve their expected life span (LawInsider.com, n.d.).

> **Operations Teams**
> Include the functions, duties, and responsibilities associated with providing integration, maintenance, and ongoing support functions.

Throughout the lifecycle, but particularly at the end of a change activity, the delivery teams work closely with the operations teams to ensure the seamless transition of the change and to position the operational organization(s) for success. To facilitate this transition, delivery teams may perform some of the following tasks:

- Preparing information for customer support. This may include escalation procedures should the change require routine or emergency attention.
- Documentation to support the change regarding its design and usage.
- Knowledge transition in terms of training the operations support teams on the change activity prior to its introduction into the production baseline.
- Support for a transition period to facilitate a smooth hand over.

In addition to the items noted above, the delivery and operations teams collaborate throughout the process— from inception and planning to design and prototyping to the eventual delivery of the change. This collaboration ensures that change item(s) consider the needs of the operations support teams and ultimately the customer. The operations teams have a unique voice in the process as they work with the customers daily and have insights that may better position the change activities for success once deployed. This insight is critical to the overall process and is the basis of the DevOps practices described earlier.

# Chapter 3:
# Program Team Roles

As described above the program team performs many functions to align the work of the delivery teams with the organizational strategy. At the beginning of the program (or when it is first established), a program charter is often developed to include program and delivery team roles and responsibilities. Depending upon the size of the program, multiple roles may be performed by a single person, or, on larger programs, individuals will focus on specific functions.

This section describes the core roles of the program management, delivery and operations teams and other roles found on many programs. The current standards including *The Standard for Program Management* (PMI, 2017) and *Managing Successful Programmes* (Axelos, 2020) define the core program management roles to include a Program Sponsor, Program Manager and PMO Lead. Based on the introduction of agile practices, and the considerations for self-organization and self-managed teams, the roles performed at the program level are changing. In the "redefined model" two additional program level roles are included, a Program Delivery Manager and Organizational Change Manager for larger programs.

The Program Delivery Manager role facilitates the alignment of efforts across the delivery and operations teams. This role has emerged as a result of Agile@Scale methods and may be performed by a Program Manager or delegated to someone else. The Organizational Change Manager role has been introduced into the "redefined" model as a program level core role based on the need to not only focus on the technical aspects of change activities, but also to focus on the people side of change. The perpetual Top Ten reasons for project failure are people oriented. Common findings including a lack of understanding of customer requirements, poor communications, the absence of stakeholder engagement, and many other failure reasons (Jacob, 2021; Stewart, 2022) that lead to outcomes that are difficult to integrate and ultimately not fully (or at all) adopted by the intended customers (Shafayet, 2022).

Other roles commonly found in Agile@Scale methods include a Chief Architect / Lead Engineer, Product Owner, and either a Project Manager or Scrum Master leading the delivery teams. The Operations team leads are also integrated into the redefined model. To reiterate an earlier point, it is important to note that there isn't necessarily a 1:1 relationship of roles to per person. Multiple roles may be performed by a single person depending upon the size and scope of the program. For example, The Program Manager, PMO Lead and Delivery Coordinator may be the same person. At least until a time that the responsibility warrants additional resources. Similarly, a single person may perform the Product Manager and Product Owner roles concurrently. Considering all the above, a potential list of roles on a program may include the following:

- Program Sponsor
- Program Manager
- Program Management Office Lead
- Program Delivery Manager
- Organizational Change Manager
- Chief Architect / Lead Engineer
- Product Manager and Product Owners

- Delivery and Operations Team Leads

With as many roles involved, it could be daunting to figure out who does what. The example that follows is intended to provide some context and will be referenced for each role introduced throughout this chapter.

In 2023, Sweden is expected to become the world's first cashless society (Swedish Institute, 2021). The move to a cashless society was partly based on the increase in counterfeit banknotes over the past few years along with advances in digitalization. As digital options have increased, Sweden's residents have embraced these options and the amount of cash in circulation has fallen over the last ten years (Sveriges Riksbank, 2020). The effort to move to a cashless society is a major undertaking not only for the Government's Central Bank, but also for Banks, Merchants, Individuals, and other parties impacted by this change. Below are just a few of the overall changes required (Fourtané, 2020):

- Create a mobile payment system (Swish) for individuals to exchange payments with friends, family and for individual transactions (e.g., purchases at the Christmas Market in Stockholm, buying a car from an individual, donating at church, etc.).

- Create a cryptocurrency (e-Krona).
- Create a nation-wide secure identity for transactions.
- Ensure all merchants only accept electronic payments (i.e., credit/debit cards, mobile payments, etc.).
- Provide currency solutions for minors.

Imagine this change is occurring in your country and you are selected as the Program Manager to lead the change activities for a large bank. You are requested to setup the program to provide governance, alignment, and support for each of the change activities described above…

## Program Sponsor

Often the first person assigned to the Cashless Program would likely be a Program Sponsor. The Program

Sponsor is the program's executive change leader who communicates the importance of the program to key stakeholders and senior leadership and obtains funding, buy in, and collaboration. The Program Sponsor is the senior business owner (and often considered the *Champion*) for the Cashless Program and has broad authority for decision-making relative to program funding, scope, direction, utilization of organizational resources, conflict resolution, and ensures the program maintains alignment with the organizational strategies throughout its life cycle. They

> **Program Sponsor** is the program's executive change leader who communicates the importance of the program to key stakeholders and senior leadership and obtains buy in and collaboration.

often identify the Program Manager and the Program Steering Committee members. In addition, they generally serve as the Chair of the Program Steering Committee meetings and maintain strategic communications with the senior and executive management between meetings.

I've personally experienced cases in which the Program Manager was the first assigned. When this happens, it is imperative for the Program Manager to identify the appropriate Program Sponsor. If you want to know who the sponsor is, "follow the money." This means finding the person who reviews and approves the allocation of resources and request their active participation or request their assistance in identifying the appropriate sponsor. Keep in mind that "management support" is often cited as a (and often the) top reason for program failure. Don't go it alone.

## Program Manager

The Cashless Program Manager has the overall responsibility for leading the program. They work closely with the Program Sponsor, Organizational Change Manager(s), Product Manager(s), and Chief

> ***Program Manager*** has the overall responsibility for leading the program. This includes securing resources to aid in providing governance, alignment, and delivery support.

Architect(s) to define the program scope, continuously reprioritize work. They establish the delivery teams and coordinate the activities amongst the same teams (Delivery Team Leads [Scrum Masters, Project Managers, etc.]) and operations team members. The core responsibilities of the Program are described earlier in Chapter 2.

In the case of preparing the bank for cashless solutions, the Program Manager will work with several business and technical teams to identify those who may lead each respective delivery and operations teams for each change area. As each delivery team is established, the program team will work with that team and others to coordinate the efforts across the organization.

## Program Management Office (PMO) Lead

The PMO lead is a critical role in supporting governance and delivery team support for the program organization. The PMO supports the program lifecycle by assisting in support for new program requests (i.e., Intake, Demand Management, Ideation), tracking throughout the lifecycle, and reporting on the outputs or outcomes (AcqNotes, 2023). While the specific roles and responsibilities are varied, they may include (Zein, 2010):

- Providing leadership for setting up tools and standards for managing the program;
- Planning, tracking, and reporting on outputs and outcomes;
- Information and logistics management;
- Financial planning and tracking; and

- Risk and Issue tracking.

The PMO lead can aid the Cashless Program in developing and sharing standards for common processes or automating routines that result in shorter cycle times and reduced costs. They also provide executive level views of the program information to aid in decision-making.

## Program Delivery Manager

The program team is responsible for aligning the efforts of the delivery team and often they use different forums depending upon their needs. Depending upon the size and complexity of the program the Program Manager themselves may facilitate Delivery Coordination meetings or identity a Program Delivery Manager to facilitate these meetings. This is not a status meeting but facilitated interactions between and among teams intended to assess new opportunities, validate priorities of upcoming change activities, coordinate cross team efforts, remove roadblocks, align organizational outputs, and record benefits achieved.

As new Agile@Scale methods emerged in 2005, new roles and responsibilities also came about. Once used primarily for cross team coordination with Agile@Scale methods, the Program Delivery Manager role has been adopted by traditional methods and non-scaled agile teams as well. As each Agile@Scale method appeared, the Program Delivery Manager role was given many different titles depending upon the Agile@Scale method being used. The role may be called:

- Senior Scrum Master (e.g., Large Scale Scrum, Scrum of Scrums, Disciplined Agile® Delivery, others);
- Tribe Leader (i.e., Spotify),
- Release Train Engineer (i.e., SAFe); and
- Service Delivery Manager (SDM), Service Request Manager (SRM), or Iteration Manager (i.e., Enterprise Kanban).

While there are some differences between the full set of responsibilities, the core functions are similar – support cross team collaboration and coordination. Regardless of the name used for the role, it is important to ensure the work is covered. A RACI Chart may be used to support this need.

For the Cashless Program, the Program Delivery Manager (or Program Manager) is responsible for cross team coordination. This may include managing communications across delivery teams, escalating risks, helping resolve cross team interdependencies, and driving continuous improvements.

## Organizational Change Manager

Programs often impact many different business areas (over time) with proposed or projected changes they are chartered to deliver. The Organizational Change Manager supports the Organizational Change Management aspects of the impending changes by working closely with business areas, program, and delivery teams to identify and prepare the impacted organizations (business, information technology, or others) for the upcoming changes to maximize employee adoption and usage of the program outcomes upon delivery to ensure the benefits are fully realized.

The Cashless Program may affect multiple areas of the bank and the person (or group of people) in this role helps ensure there is appropriate information, buy-in, planning and preparation for the changes in advance to ensure a smooth transition upon delivery. Based on the proposed changes, the Organizational Change Manager may have others assigned to support each area of organizational change. These changes may apply to business areas, information technology (often operations) areas, other business support areas (Contracts, Legal, HR, Unions, etc.) or third-party vendors (where business functions have been sourced).

In this context, there will be many process changes to support the cashless (commercial and individual) customers, transactions, and accounts. The Organizational Change Manager may engage representatives from Business, Human Capital Management (or Human Resources), Operations, Labor Unions, etc. to prepare for product or process changes, considering training, staffing, compensation, and myriad other changes.

## Chief Architect/Lead Engineer

The Cashless Program Chief Architect provides direction, guidance and advice relative to the proposed technical changes of the program. They work closely with the enterprise architecture team to ensure organizational technical alignment. They serve as the program design authority and major decision-maker by assessing technical designs and dependencies across the program. In this case, there are many potential systems impacted or new systems required. In addition, there may be external linkages (interfaces) to systems (in Sweden, Swish, elsewhere PayPal, Venmo, Zelle, Apple / Google / Samsung / Other Pay) that were not previously required. They often help facilitate brainstorming exercises to elicit options and opportunities across the delivery teams. The Chief Architect may serve as an architect, coach, or mentor (or even lead developer) on one or more delivery teams.

## Product Manager & Product Owners

Product management in organizations usually involves two key roles: the Product Manager and the Product Owner. The Product Manager role is considered strategic, as it involves market research, customer feedback, product vision, strategy and roadmapping, planning, forecasting, release management, customer understanding, requirement management, marketing, stakeholder and sales management, prioritization of requirements, budgeting, market launch, and other responsibilities (Schuurman, 2020). The Product Manager role is typically aligned with the portfolio and program teams. On the other hand, the Product Owner is aligned with the delivery teams. There may be a Product Owner for each of the Cashless Products based on customer base (commercial, personal, etc.), product set (Bank Cards [Credit, Debit], Electronic Transactions [Automated Clearing House, Third Party, Bank Owned]) or other delineation depending on how the bank is organized.

The Product Owner role relates to the work involved with the product relative to their role implementing Scrum. Among other responsibilities, the Product Owner works closely with delivery teams in an Agile environment to define the product vision by continuously reviewing the business needs and gaining stakeholder inputs, manages the product backlog by planning milestones and deliverables while identifying constraints and refining priorities, and provides oversight by identify opportunities and helping to mitigate risks (Fechter, 2021).

While the names of the titles may sound counterintuitive (i.e., Product Manager is strategic, while Product Owner is focused on product delivery), the Product Manager role was introduced well before Agile practices for software development were established. When creating roles for the Scrum Guide in the 1990s, Ken Schwaber and Jeff Sutherland chose this new name (Product Owner) to differentiate from the existing role of Product Manager (Schuurman, 2020). This involves focusing on a subset of the responsibilities shared above in their support and active participation in Scrum Teams.

The Product Manager and Product Owner could be the same person in some organizations. In larger organizations with many concurrent changes occurring across the product line(s), this may not be feasible given the commitment of time required to perform the function of a Product Owner on a Scrum team.

## Delivery and Operations Team Leads

Delivery Team may be led by Project Managers, Scrum Masters, or a Hybrid Project/Scrum Master role depending upon the work scope they are assigned to support. The scope of work for Project Managers is described in "eight performance domains that form an integrated system to enable successful delivery of the project and intended outcomes" (PMI, 2021, p. 3). The performance domains include stakeholders, team, development approach and life cycle, planning, project work, delivery, measurement, and uncertainty.

A Scrum Master is accountable for establishing Scrum as defined in the Scrum Guide. They are responsible for the Scrum Team's effectiveness through training and facilitating Scrum events (Schwaber & Sutherland, 2020). They do this by helping everyone understand Scrum theory and practice, both within the Scrum Team and the organization. Today, a Hybrid Scrum Master/PM role has emerged. We can look at the job boards for evidence of such. The job description for the role often requests those with credentials in both project management and in Scrum. In 2021, The Project Management Institute began offering the Agile Hybrid

Project Pro™ micro-credential to certify the recipient's knowledge of new PMP standards, which include Agile and Hybrid approaches (Kodwani, 2021).

The Program Manager for the Cashless Program will select Project Managers, Scrum Masters, or those with Hybrid capabilities based on their knowledge and judgment of the support required. While the delivery teams are self-managed in that they organize semi-autonomously to manage their work, they are not fully autonomous in that their work efforts are coordinated and aligned via the program (or portfolio) team. Operations leads may also be aligned directly with a program or be regarded as a significant stakeholder in the program. In either case, their inputs throughout the process are important in that the change activities from the program must be readily supported for the program to be considered truly successful.

## Other Program Roles & Responsibilities

In addition to the roles above, in larger programs some of the work of the program management team may be distributed to individuals to perform specific functions. Depending upon the size and scope of the program, the program team may be comprised of team members with specific responsibilities as listed below:

- Program Communications
- Quality Management
- Program Information Management
- Program Risk/Issue Management
- Resource Management and Program Support (Procurement, Legal, Vendor Management, Financial Management, etc.)
- Learning and Development

The specific responsibilities and techniques for each practice area are covered later in this book.

# Part II:
# The Origin of
# Agile Practices

# Part II:

# The Origin of Agile

# Practices

Agile practices in use today have emerged based on a confluence of changes in Organizational Design theory (largely initially focused on manufacturing industries), the concepts of organizational agility, the application of that theory to software development (pre-Manifesto), values and principles from the Manifesto for Agile Software Development, and several other contributing methods, frameworks, and practices (see Figure 3). This section describes the core and contributing influences that helped shape the practices presented later in this book.

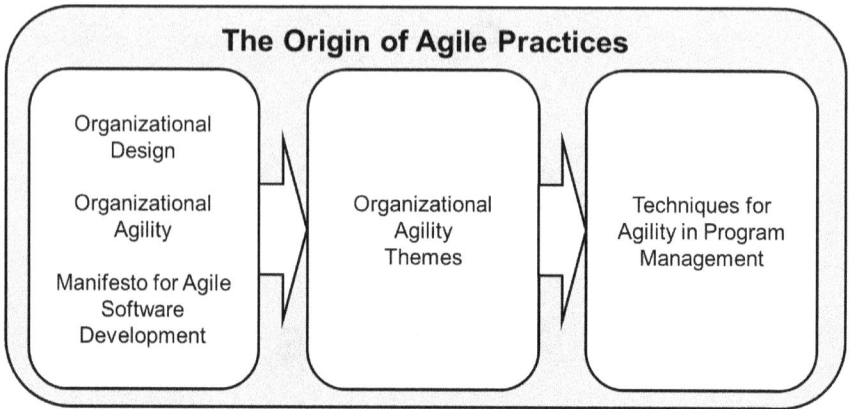

*Figure 3.* Agile practices today are rooted in many foundational disciplines, methods, and frameworks culminating in techniques for agility in Program Management.

In the chapters that follow, the core disciplines of Organizational Design Theory, Organizational Agility, and the Manifesto for Agile Software Development are presented. Each chapter includes a brief historical perspective and an overview of each discipline. Several themes emerged based on a review of these disciplines. A chapter on Organizational Agility Themes shares considerations and potential practices to be applied to Program Management. These practices are in part derived from the disciplines and from the values and principles from the Manifesto for Agile Software Development. This common set of themes can be applied to Program Management or other disciplines as appropriate. Finally, Part III aligns these organizational agility themes with techniques for agility in Program Management for the practitioner to consider while performing their responsibilities across the life cycle.

# Chapter 4:
# Organizational Design

Organizational design topologies have changed over the years and the associated management structure and practices across have evolved as well. Practices developed for manufacturing and construction industries have been applied to all types of organizations and industries over time. Agile practices in use today are rooted in these organizational design approaches and can be traced back more recently to methods and practices used in the software industry. Figure 4 summarizes the organizational design topology and associated features and the software development methods in use over time.

| Timeline | Predictive (Plan Driven) up to 1970 | Iterative / Incremental 1970s – 1980s | 1980s – 2000 | Adaptive (Change Driven) 2000-today |
|---|---|---|---|---|
| Org Design | Rational | Natural | Open | Complex Adaptive |
| Attributes | Formal, Structured, Sequential, Standardized, Plan driven | Collaborative, Plan to Change driven | Integrated, Change to Value driven, Non-linear, Emergent | Self-organizing, non-linear, and emergent structures, responsive to environmental changes |
| Popular Software Development Methods | Waterfall (1956); Structured Programming (1964); Cap Gemini SDM (1970); | JAD (1974); V-Model (1979); SSADM (1980); RAD (1981); SW Prototyping (1983); Spiral (1986) | Scrum (1986); Crystal (1991); DSDM (1994); SoS (1996); FDD (1997); RUP (1998); XP (1999) | LeSS (2005); DAD (2007); SAFe® (2011); Spotify (2012); RAGE (2013), Nexus™ (2015). |

*Figure 4.* Software development methods changed over time in response to new management approaches.

## Rational Systems Organizational Design

Adam Smith first wrote about the efficiencies gained by the division of labor and worker specialization in his 1776 book *An Inquiry into the Nature and Causes of the Wealth of Nations*. This early organizational design structure was later described as a *Rational or Closed Systems*, where the work was performed in a formal, structured, top-down hierarchy and workers perfected their craft by focusing in specific areas and experimenting to improve the processes resulting in higher productivity. In the early-1900s, Frederick Taylor, Max Weber, and Henri Fayol expanded upon these theories. However, there was much pushback from the workforce as they felt dehumanized and treated like machines. Despite the pushback, core elements of this approach were largely followed for the next 50+ years.

> **Rational Systems**
> Characterized by having formal, structured, top-down hierarchy and workers perfected their craft by focusing in specific areas and experimenting to improve the processes resulting in higher productivity.

Early software development methods in the 1950s through the 1970s--most notably Waterfall (Herbert

Benington's 1956 model for manufacturing and construction projects)— reflected this closed system management approach where all the work was planned up front and then each step (system requirements, software requirements, analysis, program design, coding, testing, operations [Royce, 1970]) was performed in sequence, focusing on each area of specialization, and completing each step before moving to the next.

While this new approach offered more control than earlier ad hoc methods, a central problem is that the scope of work is determined at the onset of the program; and those fixed requirements are cascaded throughout the life cycle. A core problem with the method was there was an assumption that once the requirements were defined, there would be no need to accommodate changes to this fixed scope. This did not come to fruition in most real-world situations. In addition, there was little collaboration between functional teams (requirements analysts, designers, developers, etc.), and much emphasis was placed on developing comprehensive documentation in the form of turnover packages. Once the software was ready, in many cases, the needs of the business had changed significantly, creating the need for considerable rework.

This would be like starting a business to build outdoor playhouses. You start by building your first one for your two children. You research specialists you can work with to complete the stages of the build. You bring in an analyst to write up the requirements. Months pass and you then package and send these requirements to a specialist at a building design firm to draw up a design (without consulting your spouse or the children). More time passes and you finally receive the design. Now you contact a general contractor (another specialist) to order and wait for the materials to arrive. Finally, they (the GC) contract a builder to begin to construct the playhouse.

Three years have now passed, and your children are ready to begin playing in it. The trouble is, you now have four children, the ceiling isn't high enough for the eldest, the space is too small to house all of them and their friends, the technology is dated, and décor doesn't match this new group of stakeholders. Over time, the requirements changed, and the sequential nature of your process didn't account for your *customer's future needs*.

## Natural Systems Organizational Design

In the 1970 and 1980s organizations began employing a *Natural Systems* management approach. This approach arose in response to the limitations and impacts on workers of *Rational Systems* approaches where top-down

> **Natural Systems**
> Characterized by a human centered approach with methods focused on taking on smaller increments of work and allowing for change to emerge.

structures and little interaction between workers proved inefficient. The emergence of a human-centered approach at this time and is largely attributed to the work of Australian George Elton Mayo (along with Fritz Roethlisberger, T.N. Whitehead, and William Dickson) in his involvement in a series of human research projects at the Western Electric Company, Hawthorne Works, outside of Chicago (Jenkins, 1940). The results from these studies quickly made their way to other industries as new collaborative methods emerged. Software development methods including Joint Application Development, Rapid Application Development and Spiral Development methods (among others) began the movement away from only waterfall methods and placed a premium on working together and sharing information in smaller teams. These methods focused on taking on smaller increments of work and allowing for change to emerge. While the benefits of collaboration and shortened development cycles proved effective, the management approach was still largely internally focused. The voice of the customer and other stakeholders wasn't fully integrated or in some cases even considered.

Using this approach with the outdoor playhouse, you've consulted your spouse and children in the design at the beginning, and all are happy. You hire a small team to construct this and other outdoor playhouses. You build it faster; however, your internal focus didn't account for the Homeowners Association being stakeholders. Their restriction on stand-alone structures means you cannot keep it outside, not to mention the local building codes. So, you may either place it in the basement (unless you live in an area where there are not basements [e.g., Florida]) or you must physically connect it to your house.

## Open Systems Organizational Design

*Open Systems* models arose from biological and ecological research where organisms were found as interconnected and mutually influential. Open Systems models emerged in the software industry in response to changes in the overall landscape in the 1990s. In the early years of software, companies primarily developed software solutions specific to their individual needs. Over the years, many new companies were founded

> **Open Systems**
> An organization design construct characterized by considering the interdependent nature of systems being interconnected and mutually influential.

to develop solutions for common processes (e.g., Human Resources, Finance, Supply Chain, etc.) and others arose to meet the ever-increasing demand for businesses to expand upon or modernize their existing baseline. Whether writing software for others or internally, the significant backlog of customer requirements necessitated a new approach.

"Agile" methods began to emerge to address the need to sense and respond to customer needs. New prioritization methods and roles also emerged. Early on, Agile Methods focused on small teams of developers to quickly turn around customer requests in an iterative manner in two week "sprints" vs. multi-year plans. Scrum, Crystal, Extreme Programming, Rational Unified Process, and other methods took hold, each with a focus on rapid development cycles and customer centricity.

Finally, your company has three divisions: Outdoor Playhouses, Tool Sheds and Music Studios. One team (Outdoor Playhouses) uses a prioritized list of features when building the outdoor playhouse. They build the structure onsite in small increments prioritizing the frame and roof with constant collaboration with the stakeholders. The children are happy because they can use it early in the process and they had input into the design along the way. The Homeowner's Association was consulted, so you built it into the design to have it attached to the back of the house, so it wasn't free standing or visible by the neighbors. Only problem is now, your other two divisions still follow the old approach, and more and more customers are requesting custom features. How do you share best practices and scale across your business to accommodate custom features based on this expanded stakeholder community? If you don't figure it out, your competitors will.

## Complex Adaptive Systems Organizational Design

Modern organizational designs are built upon

complexity theories that study natural systems like brains, immune systems, ecologies, and societies, as well as artificial systems such as parallel and distributed computing systems, artificial intelligence systems, artificial neural networks, and evolutionary programs. These

> **Complex Adaptive Systems**
> Characterized by concepts of self-organization, non-linearity, emergence, and responsiveness.

theories, known as "complex adaptive systems," were first developed in the early 1980s at the Santa Fe Institute in New Mexico, USA, to describe how the living world operates. Today, we can apply Complex Adaptive Systems (CAS) theory to discuss Agile practices used in software development at scale. CAS theory encompasses the concepts of self-organization, non-linearity, emergence, and responsiveness, which are all attributes of a CAS.

As with the earlier methods, considering the desire to leverage both the considerations of Complex Adaptive systems into their management structure and to take advantage of the success of Agile methodologies, organizations sought to scale Agile methods from small teams to apply the principles and practices at the organization level in the early 2000s.

The first Large-Scale Agile method, Large Scale Scrum, was introduced in 2005 to coordinate between agile teams. Since then, additional models were introduced to support: larger team size, geographical distribution, regulatory compliance, organizational distribution, technical complexity, domain complexity, organizational complexity, and enterprise discipline (Ambler, 2010). Several Large-Scale Agile methods are in use today (e.g., Disciplined Agile, Dynamic Systems Delivery Method [DSDM], Large Scale Scrum [LeSS], Scaled Agile Framework® [SAFe], Nexus Framework, Recipes for Agile Governance in the Enterprise ™ [RAGE], Scrum of Scrums [SoS], Scaling Agile @ Spotify [Spotify Model]), each with the goal of quickly responding to organizational change but at a scale larger with many of the models leveraging the Agile methods at the team level.

The Outdoor Building Corporation (www.OBC.idk) is now fully operational, and you have managed to standardize practices throughout your expanding company. Instead of having three divisions, you now have one that handles all builds, regardless of their purpose or customization. Although you have locations across the globe, your prefabricated products are customizable through your website and made from locally sourced, eco-friendly, sustainable, and lightweight materials. Additionally, a range of standard products is available through big-box and home improvement stores. You can manufacture a large number of products quickly, and they can be shipped to your new global customer base within a few days, requiring minimal assembly. Fortune magazine has taken notice of your impressive scaling, and they want to know your secret.

# Chapter 5:

# Organizational Agility

As discussed in an earlier section, since the dawn of the industrial age, businesses have constantly sought opportunities to increase output, improve quality, stave off competitors, and increase their profitability.

> **Organizational Agility**
> Largely defined by five core capabilities: responsiveness, competency, flexibility, speed, and stakeholder satisfaction.

As the Information Age took form in the mid-20th century, new opportunities emerged to use technology as a strategic asset in meeting these goals. Both businesses and academic institutions sought to find the common elements supporting the earlier stated goals. This section discusses two notable initiatives to define agility that came from The University of California, Marshall School of Business, and the Iacocca Institute at Lehigh University.

## Organizational Agility Profiler

In 1979, the Center for Effective Organizations (CEO) was established at University of California's Marshall School of Business. To better understand the criteria that makes an organization successful, they studied performance data from 243 large firms in 17 industries over the 30-year period from 1979 to 2009 (Williams, Worley & Lawler, 2014). As a result of their research, the authors developed a "short survey" that is used to gauge an organization's agility based on their response to 19 survey questions in a questionnaire (see Appendix C) the authors entitled the "Organizational Agility Profiler" (Worley, Williams, and Lawler, 2014).

The Organizational Agility Profiler survey is based on the research of Worley, Williams, and Lawler (2014) documented in their book *Assessing your organization's agility: Creating diagnostic profiles to guide transformation*. The survey is based upon four "routines" of agility (see Figure 5) that distinguish outperformers from underperformers. Questions related to each routine are provided in Figure 5.

| Routine | Description |
|---|---|
| Strategizing | How top management teams establish an aspirational purpose, develop a widely shared strategy, and manage the climate and commitment to execution. |
| Perceiving | The process of broadly, deeply, and continuously, monitoring the environment to sense changes and rapidly communicate these perceptions to decision makers, who interpret and formulate appropriate responses. |
| Testing | How the organization sets up, runs, and learns from experiments. |
| Implementing | How the organization maintains its ability and capacity to implement changes, both incremental and discontinuous, as well as its ability to verify the contribution of execution to performance. |

*Figure 5.* The Routines of Agility. (Worley, Williams & Lawler, 2014, p. 27).

Each of the routines described above can be measured as independent variables, with an equal weight attribution to the dependent variable, organizational agility (see Figure 6). The calculations and survey are provided in Appendix C. Scores above 2.75 are generally higher than the baseline. Scores closer to 4 in each area are relatively "more agile" where lower scores indicate "less agile." For more information, please refer to the book: *Assessing Organization Agility: Creating Diagnostic Profiles to Guide Transformation* which can be found on Amazon.com.

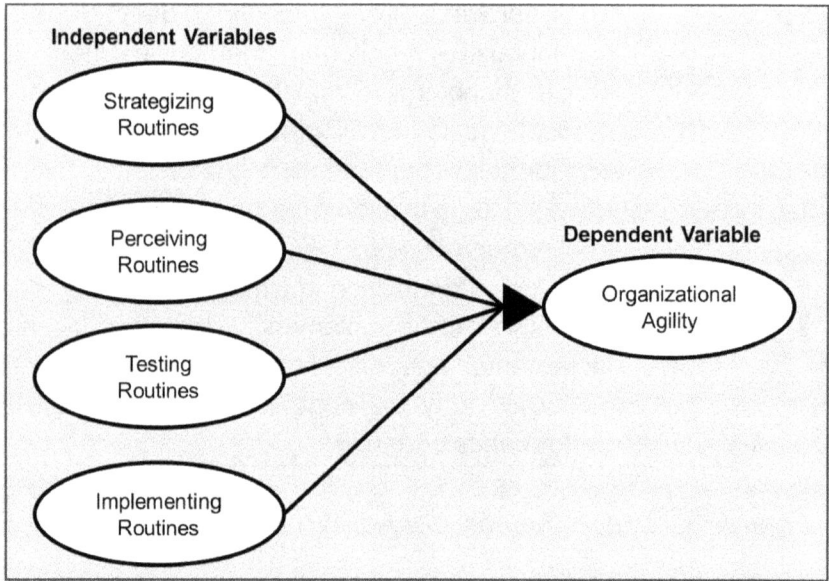

*Figure 6.* Organizational Agility Variables. Adapted with permission from *The Agility Factor: Building Adaptable Organizations for Superior Performance*, by Worley, C. G., Williams, T., Lawler, E. E., 2014, San Francisco, CA, Jossey-Bass.

The questions used in the survey can provide insight into the *perception* of those in the organization on their current level of organizational agility. The survey is meant to be periodically repeated after implementing changes in areas that require attention, while considering the inherent potential bias of the survey respondents.

## Agile Manufacturing

The term, "Agile Manufacturing" was popularized in 1991 by a group of scholars at the Iacocca Institute of Lehigh University who defined it as: "… a manufacturing system with extraordinary capabilities (Internal capabilities: hard and soft technologies, human resources, educated management, information) to meet the rapidly changing needs of the marketplace (speed, flexibility, customers, competitors, suppliers, infrastructure, responsiveness). A system that shifts quickly (speed and responsiveness) among product models or between product lines (flexibility), ideally in real-time response to customer demand (customer needs and wants)" (Yusuf, Sarhadi, & Gunasekaran, 1999).

## Defining Organizational Agility

The term "Organizational Agility" was soon after used to apply this concept to other industries. Organizational agility was defined as "the result of integrating alertness to changes (recognizing opportunities/challenges) – both internal and environmental – with a capability to use resources in responding (proactive/responsive) to such changes, all in a timely, flexible, affordable, relevant manner" (Alzoubi, Al-otoum, & Albatainh, 2011, p. 505). As discussed in the prior section, organizational agility is closely tied to the Complex Adaptive System (CAS) theory elements of responsiveness and emergence. In a CAS, there is no separation between a system and its environment in that a system always adapts to a changing environment (Chan, 2001).

There have been many attempts to define a common approach to measuring organizational agility. Roy Wendler (2013) reviewed 28 frameworks of agility and concluded "there is absolutely no consensus of what really constitutes the construct of agility" (p. 165). Yauch (2011) found that organizational agility models differ in numerous ways where some: relate to specific business processes, emphasize agility across supply chains, focus on individual business units, and others focus on internal operational measures.

Despite these concerns, there is consensus regarding the importance of organization's ability to sense and respond to changes in the environment. Based on the two studies listed above and information from the review of several other sources, organizational agility capabilities largely consider the five core capabilities of responsiveness, competency, flexibility, speed, and stakeholder satisfaction. While listed separately, each capability is often intertwined with one another. The resultant themes are included in Part III where Organizational Agility Themes are applied to program management practices.

# Chapter 6:

# The Agile Manifesto

In the mid to late 1980s, the first "agile" methods were emerging in the software industry. Agile methods, as the name implies, were introduced to increase organizational agility by supporting the need to respond quickly to change and minimize rework and structural delays found in traditional methods. Using Agile methods, the full software development lifecycle is performed by a small collaborative work team, generally smaller than 15 people (Ambler, 2010). Today, a common heuristic for the team size is seven +/- two team members (between five and nine). These self-managed and self-organized teams develop software incrementally in short, time-boxed development cycles or "sprints." They prioritize features and focus on delivering the highest priority features in one- to six-week increments, with two-week sprints being common.,

Many of the methods presented earlier in Figure 4 have evolved and are in use today by Information Technology, Financial Services, Professional Services, Insurance, Government, Healthcare and Pharmaceutical, Industrial/Manufacturing, Telecommunications, Energy, Education, Retail, Transportation, Media/Entertainment and Non-profit industries (CollabNet, 2019). While the early adopters experienced success, most organizations at that time were only experimenting with "agile" methods, most were using Waterfall as their primary method.

## Agile Values and Principles

In 2001, a group of seventeen software development industry experts (developers, methodologists, authors, and others) convened to define values and principles of agility to apply to software development. Many of the participants created or significantly contributed to the early agile methods mentioned earlier. The result of this gathering was a set of four core values (see Figure 7) and twelve principles (Figure 8) collectively today known as the *Agile Manifesto*.

---

# Manifesto for Agile Software Development

We are uncovering better ways of developing
software by doing it and helping others do it.
Through this work we have come to value:

**Individuals and interactions** over processes and tools
**Working software** over comprehensive documentation
**Customer collaboration** over contract negotiation
**Responding to change** over following a plan

That is, while there is value in the items on
the right, we value the items on the left more.

| | | |
|---|---|---|
| Kent Beck | James Grenning | Robert C. Martin |
| Mike Beedle | Jim Highsmith | Steve Mellor |
| Arie van Bennekum | Andrew Hunt | Ken Schwaber |
| Alistair Cockburn | Ron Jeffries | Jeff Sutherland |
| Ward Cunningham | Jon Kern | Dave Thomas |
| Martin Fowler | Brian Marick | |

---

*Figure 7.* The Agile Values. Reprinted from "Manifesto for Agile Software Development," by Beck et al., 2001, Agile Alliance, http://agilemanifesto.org/.

Some of the original authors of the Manifesto and others agreed that additional benefit could be derived by having a more permanent organization than just the initial meeting where the Manifesto was created. Based on this the Agile Alliance (AgileAlliance.org) was formed in late 2001. The Agile Alliance is a nonprofit organization that today has over 72,000 members with a charter to "support people and organizations who explore, apply and expand Agile values, principles, and practices" (Agile Alliance, 2022).

Early interpretations of the intent of the values were mixed. Some saw the values as Boolean comparisons, meaning only the one on the left was important. The authors provided some insight into their goals by the words they chose to introduce the values. "Uncovering" implied the journey has not been completed, the authors "don't have all the answers and don't subscribe to the silver-bullet theory" (Fowler & Highsmith, 2001). Subsequent articles and conference presentations were also developed to help allay concerns and misconceptions and clarify the intent.

Since its publication in 2001, the four Agile values and 12 Agile principles have been widely adopted beyond software development and applied to various business and information technology activities in government, non-profit, and commercial organizations.

---

**Principles behind the Agile Manifesto**

We follow these principles:

- Our highest priority is to satisfy the customer through early and continuous delivery of valuable software.
- Welcome changing requirements, even late in development. Agile processes harness change for the customer's competitive advantage.
- Deliver working software frequently, from a couple of weeks to a couple of months, with a preference to the shorter timescale.
- Businesspeople and developers must work together daily throughout the project.
- Build projects around motivated individuals. Give them the environment and support they need and trust them to get the job done.
- The most efficient and effective method of conveying information to and within a development team is face-to-face conversation.
- Working software is the primary measure of progress.
- Agile processes promote sustainable development. The sponsors, developers, and users should be able to maintain a constant pace indefinitely.
- Continuous attention to technical excellence and good design enhances agility.
- Simplicity--the art of maximizing the amount of work not done--is essential.
- The best architectures, requirements, and designs emerge from self-organizing teams.
- At regular intervals, the team reflects on how to become more effective, then tunes and adjusts its behavior accordingly.

---

*Figure 8.* The Agile Principles. Reprinted from "Manifesto for Agile Software Development.," by Beck et al., 2001, Agile Alliance, http://agilemanifesto.org/.

Program Management Redefined

# Chapter 7:
# Organizational Agility
# Themes

To fully achieve organizational agility, organizations need to be prepared to have their teams think differently, ask difficult questions, and apply new principles and practices that lead to agility. This cultural shift may represent a new way of thinking and must permeate all levels of the organization and all functions being performed. The changes (if required) are often found in the cultural areas below:

- Team Empowerment and Servant Leadership,
- Trust and Transparency,
- Collaboration,
- Innovation through Experimentation, and
- Eagerly embracing and adopting change.

Each of these cultural elements are considered within teams and amongst teams (including management) often with internal and external customers. These areas are covered in greater detail in Parts III-V.

Changing from traditional methods to Agile and/or Agile@Scale methods may potentially pose a significant change for some organizations. Despite the effort required to transition to agile, numerous studies have shown the payoff to be well worthwhile. 18F (short for their location 1800 F Street Washington, DC) is a U.S. Government agency. Their purpose is to deliver digital services and information technology products. In their open-source Agile guide, they shared a view on Agile depicted on the right.

> **Agile is something you are, not something you do.**
>
> If you take nothing else from all these words, take this. Agile is not a checklist, or a methodology, or a series of rituals. Agile is a way of thinking and a way of attacking problems. Embrace mistakes, learn, and keep trying. Mess up and learn again and again and again. Cut your losses. Fail forward fast. It's okay. You won't get fired. You're learning.
>
> *That* is Agile.
>
> (Agile. 18F.Gov)

This statement is core to the cultural shift those in the *agile community* are espousing. The "L" is learning, not loss; innovation requires experimentation. I also understand this to mean that Agile *in and of itself* is not a method; however, practices can be derived from the values, guiding principles, definitions, and other guidance found in methods, frameworks, and processes that can be applied to Program Management.

Based on a review of the guidance found earlier in Part II, five themes have emerged that can be used to craft practices for practitioners to support organizational agility. Considering Complex Adaptive Systems theory, Organizational Agility, the Organizational Agility Profiler, and the Agile Manifesto several themes emerged. These include:

- **Organizational Competency:** The internal capabilities include the proper allocation of management, human resources, technologies, and information;
- **Market and Stakeholder Understanding:** Capabilities to sense and proactively prepare for changes in the environment. The market includes

considering internal and external customers, suppliers, and competitors;

- **Strategic Alignment and Responsiveness:** The ability to strategically align the organization with changes in the environment;

- **Structural Flexibility:** Internal structures and culture that enable resources (e.g., financial, facilities, human, material, technology, etc.) to be easily applied as changes emerge; and

- **Learning and Adaptability:** The ability to learn from experiments and quickly apply changes to continuously deliver on time to meet current needs.

To support these themes, there is an underlying need for true sponsorship where leadership support is provided via active participation in these areas. Moving to a redefined model *may* require a significant investment and cultural change to fully realize the intended benefits of this approach. Each of the five themes presented above are applied to specific techniques for the program delivery support practices presented in Parts III and IV. Additional considerations for each theme follow.

## Organizational Competency

The proper allocation of management, human resources, technologies, and other resources requires an understanding of the work environment (i.e., culture) and work required for a single or group of change activities across the program. Often specialty skills are centrally managed external to the program and resources are assigned to change activities on an as needed basis through a request (or ticketing) process. The shared resources model may work well when the expertise required is for single task or short-term support, however, this model breaks down when the skills required are core to the change activity.

For example, for a cloud migration program, there may be many change activities that require a firewall expert to assess and apply the appropriate controls to support this work. In the shared services model, there may be some wait time to write and submit a request, and a wait for a resource to be assigned based on SLAs, considering this team supports multiple change activities across multiple programs. Once the resource is assigned, time to gain context, assess, design, plan and deploy the change must be considered. If this resource was dedicated to the program, much of the wait time could be eliminated. When assessing change activities, it may be advantageous to consider the case above (and others like it) and have resources assigned to the overall program (if the workload warrants) to minimize the associated wait time.

## Market and Stakeholder Understanding

The ability to sense and respond to changing customer needs is critical to the ongoing sustainability of an organization. Programs contribute to the organization's knowledge base by collecting emerging requirements that they receive through multiple channels including press releases, news feeds, social media, websites, program, and delivery teams' interactions with internal customers teams (at all levels), and discussions with potential and current external customers, suppliers, and competitors. The program team captures and if needed presents this information to the portfolio team to jointly assess and determine the appropriate course of action based on this information to ensure the organization, at a minimum, provides competitive services and solutions, but more importantly innovates and is seen as the leader in their respective field.

There are multiple opportunities to consider integrating the changes based on the information received through various channels, depending upon the scope of the change. Delivery teams may prioritize the change and place it in the appropriate delivery (release) cycle. If the scope of change requires a new delivery effort, the program team will review and assess the priority against strategic goals and current work and take the appropriate action. If the scope necessitates, the portfolio team may need to create a new program or expand the scope of an existing program to deliver on the required change.

## Strategic Alignment and Responsiveness

As discussed above, when changes are considered based on the areas of input, the program first quickly assesses the potential change against their strategic goals. If the change is significant the program team presents this information to the portfolio team for consideration in the current program or to be facilitated in a different way. This may require a new program or additional delivery teams within that same program.

Responsiveness to the potential opportunity is paramount. The program must have in place the capability to assess new opportunities and forums to share these on a frequent basis with the appropriate stakeholders. The format for the presentation of a new opportunity is generally provided using a business case template. A business case is not required to be a heavyweight or voluminous document. At the delivery team level, a User Story is essentially a lightweight business case and based on the work proposed, may provide the appropriate level of information. A User Story is a short, simple description of a feature told from the perspective of the person who desires the new capability, usually a user or customer of the system. User stories typically follow a simple template: As a < type of user >, I want < some goal > so that < some reason > (Cohn, 2022). Acceptance criteria is also presented.

### *Business Case Development*

When the opportunity requires significant investment or poses considerable change, a business case that *briefly* states the following may be needed:

- The business problem or opportunity;
- Benefits to the organization and stakeholders (including customers, etc.);

- Risks (of pursuing and risk of not pursuing);
- Costs;
- Timelines;
- Alternatives;
- Potential technical solutions;
- Operational and customer impacts; and
- The program organization's current capability to deliver or additional resources required to deliver on the proposed change(s).

The proposed change is evaluated in relation to strategic goals and assigned an appropriate priority. In certain cases, the proposal may be rejected if it does not align with the strategy, if other initiatives already offer a similar capability, or if factors such as cost, risk, or imputed value do not justify the investment in that change.

> **Business Case** *briefly* states the business problem or opportunity, benefits, risks, cost, timeline, alternatives, potential technical solutions, operational and customer impacts and the program organization's current capability to deliver or additional resources required to deliver on the proposed change.

## Structural Flexibility

As programs can have a multi-year life cycle, it's crucial to organize program and delivery teams in a collaborative and flexible way that allows for changes as the organizational strategy evolves. The ability to sense and respond to these changes requires the capability to apply and move, as required, resources (e.g., financial, facilities, human, material, technology, etc.) to be easily migrated to the highest priority changes as they emerge. Continuous reprioritization and a focus on organizational change management are critical to support this need and are a foundational practice in the Program Delivery Framework.

There are many ways to structure a program. Over the past 20+ years, numerous models, frameworks, toolkits, and practices have emerged to support this need. These include various models for "Agile@Scale" or "Scaling Agile" Frameworks. This book uses the former term, Agile@Scale, to describe these constructs. Considerations for Agile@Scale are presented later in the Program Delivery Lifecycle chapter.

## Learning and Adaptability

Programs generally deliver changes that are unique to that organization. While the change may have been performed internally elsewhere within that organization or externally with another organization, the changes proposed may be unique in that this group of stakeholders is different, or the organization environment differs in other ways. There are a multitude of potential solutions that may be applied to support a business need or organizational strategy. There are also many cases where the changes are truly unique based on innovations or applications that haven't been previously considered. In all cases presented above, there is an inherent level of risk and uncertainty present in these programs.

At the on-set of a new change activity, a proof of concept (POC) or prototype may be created to serve as a learning platform to reduce uncertainty and subsequently, lower the risk exposure. Not all changes require a custom solution, in many cases, various Cloud based, Software as a Service (SaaS) products may be considered to solve the business needs. The program team must provide the opportunity to learn from these experiments and account for these opportunities in all aspects of their delivery support (including timelines, budgets, resource allocation, etc.). Also, during an existing delivery, considering the uncertainty of the changes, alternatives may be investigated to properly support the desired business results. It is important to maintain a culture where the inquisitive can try, fail, and try again to promote innovation and produce strategic results for the program and the larger organization. The outcomes may also have a cascading impact on the overall direction of the program. New delivery teams may be setup while existing delivery teams may be reallocated based on the findings supporting the new direction. The adaptability to change and practices to support that need is a core tenant in the redefined program management model.

These five core themes, along with areas of inquiry from the Organizational Agility Profiler, guiding principles from the Agile Manifesto, and other inputs were used in the creation of the Program Delivery Framework presented in Part III. The themes are also aligned to the *techniques for agility* subsections in each respective program practice.

# Chapter 8:

# Program Management & Agile/Agile@Scale

Program management, Agile, and Agile@Scale methods live in harmony with one another every day. One has not replaced the other. They each provide complementary methods and practices to aid organizations in achieving their strategic goals. In fact, on the SAFe® website there is a statement regarding the Release Train Engineer that states "a program manager often plays this role (Scaled Agile Inc., 2023e)." In Disciplined Agile, there is an entire page devoted to the role of the Program Manager in this Agile@Scale method (PMI, 2023b).

We have seen over the years with Agile methods at the delivery team level that there have been changes in the way software (and many other) projects are managed. And as organizations begin leveraging Agile@Scale vs Agile only at the team level, we are now seeing changes that require greater coordination, communication, and collaboration across the teams and across the organization.

## Program Management & Agile

Programs have supported delivery teams that have been using Agile methods, frameworks, and toolsets for decades to facilitate the delivery of an organization's desired business outcomes. The introduction of Agile Methods ushered in some new roles, most notably, the Scrum Master. Organizations have embraced this new role to focus on the facilitation of Scrum ceremonies. While this provided an opportunity, it also exposed some gaps between Scrum Master's responsibilities and those functions traditionally performed by those in a Project Manager role.

As an example, Program A employs Scrum Masters to facilitate Scrum Ceremonies on delivery teams, however, they are not requested to manage budgets, risks and issues, resource plans, metrics, and reporting (outside of agile measures) and other traditional project management tasks.

To close this gap, the program and delivery teams discuss the strategies and responsibilities. Some tasks may be taken up at the delivery team level by having a Project Manager perform these tasks for multiple delivery teams. Others may request these tasks be performed by the program team. Today, we are seeing this as a gap in some organizations, and in others the delivery team has combined these functions with a hybrid PM/Scrum Master role.

## Program Management & Agile@Scale

From an Agile@Scale and Program Management perspective, each of the disciplines are related in that they both involve managing multiple teams and coordinating their efforts to achieve a common goal. However, there are some key differences in their approach and scope. Agile@Scale includes frameworks, methods, and toolsets (e.g., Disciplined Agile, Dynamic Systems Delivery Method [DSDM], Large Scale Scrum [LeSS], Scaled Agile Framework® [SAFe], Nexus Framework, Recipes for Agile Governance in the Enterprise ™ [RAGE], Scrum of Scrums

[SoS], Scaling Agile @ Spotify [Spotify Model]) for managing complex initiatives that builds on the principles of agile software development. Each focus on delivering value incrementally, through the collaborative efforts of self-organized, self-managed, and cross-functional teams.

Program management is also focused on coordinating the efforts of multiple teams to achieve organizational goals. Program managers meet these goals by providing governance, strategic alignment, and delivery support to the teams as required. The program roles are often found within the methods frameworks and toolsets. Where not specifically called out, any gaps should be addressed and closed to ensure the organizational goals are achieved. One key difference between Agile@Scale and Program Management is found in that program teams provide governance. Programs support the (COBIT 2019) requirement to separate governance from management to ensure an independent and accountable group (Program team) or person (e.g., Program Manager or Program Sponsor) provides oversight to ensure risks are appropriately managed, work is strategically aligned, and progress is proceeding as planned. This is not a function of a delivery team.

# Program Management & Agile@Scale Practices

The program management practices provided in the Program Delivery Framework found in Part III of this book can be used to compare against any selected Agile@Scale method, framework, or toolset to determine if any gaps exist. Considering the program team often stands up, secures funding, and supports the delivery teams, it is at this point that the responsibilities should be aligned. To support this need it is important for the teams to communicate, collaborate and take advantage of the strengths of each discipline to determine the appropriate roles and responsibilities for providing oversight, alignment, and support to deliver incremental value for the sponsoring organization. This should all be done while maximizing resources and supporting self-managed, semi-autonomous teams as appropriate.

# Part III:
# Program
# Delivery
# Framework

# Part III:

# Program Delivery

# Framework

The Program Delivery Framework provides a comprehensive and simplified framework for managing programs. The framework is guided by three core practice areas and three guiding principles that are shown in Figure 9.

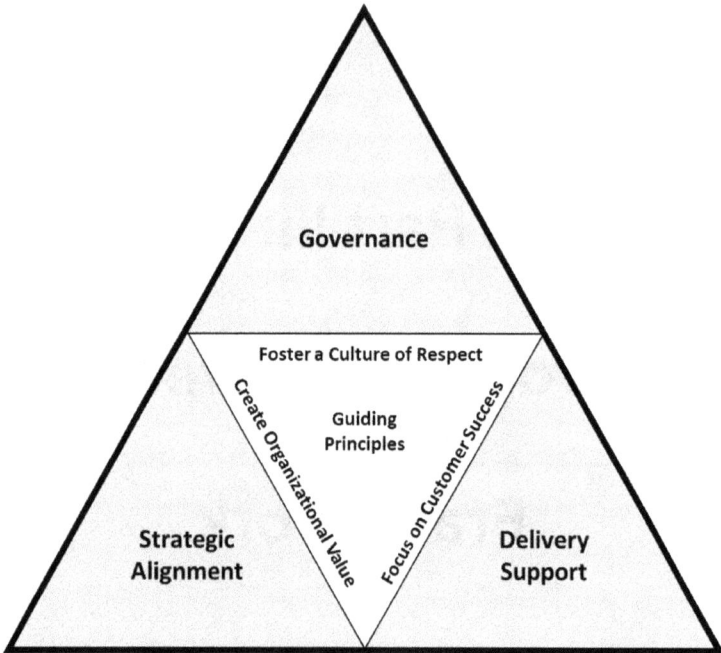

*Figure 9*: The guidance for the Program Delivery Framework consists of three core practice areas and three guiding principles.

The core practice areas, Governance, Strategic Alignment, and Delivery Support are ubiquitous throughout the program, and each have supporting practices that are performed across the program lifecycle. The first two core practice areas, Governance and Strategic Alignment, are discussed in this section (Part III) and Delivery Support is covered in Part V along with the program lifecycle and program outcomes. The first two core practice areas (Governance and Strategic Alignment) are also program practices, with Delivery Support being further divided into seven primary and three supporting program practices (see Part IV). The Program Delivery Life cycle includes three phases in which the delivery practices are performed. Program outcomes are the net expected results/benefits the program is chartered to achieve. The delivery lifecycle and outcomes are presented in Part V.

Guiding principles represent the core values and operating culture to guide the program and associated organizations throughout the lifecycle *in all circumstances, irrespective of changes in its goals, strategies, type of work or the top management* (Mathenge & Stevens-Hall, 2019). The guiding principles shown in Figure 9 are covered in detail later in Chapter 10. The full Program Delivery Framework is presented in Chapter 9.

# Chapter 9:
# Program Delivery
# Framework

The Program Delivery Framework (see Figure 10) represents a redefined model for program management. This framework considers practices for organizational agility, current and emerging management practices, and insights from this author and others I've collaborated with based on our collective experiences in leading complex programs. It also recognized the changes and opportunities that have emerged as organizations adopt agile methods at the enterprise, portfolio, program, and delivery team level. The framework was developed to help organizations:

- Improve alignment;
- Enhance visibility of work-in-progress;

- Improve stakeholder collaboration;
- Manage organizational risks;
- Increase efficiency;
- Increase agility;
- Reduce costs; and
- Improve Return on Investment (ROI).

This is performed by coordinating resources (e.g., financial, facilities, human, material, technology, etc.) across multiple teams while delivering on strategic objectives.

The framework is comprised of four general sections. On the far left are Guiding Principles and Core Practice Areas (denoted as #1). These provide core management considerations and guidance for the overall program. Guiding Principles are presented in this section (Chapter 10), and the Core Practice Areas that include Governance and Strategic Alignment are discussed in Chapters 11 and 12, respectively. Another Core Practice Area, Delivery Support, is presented in the Program Delivery Support Practices section in Part IV.

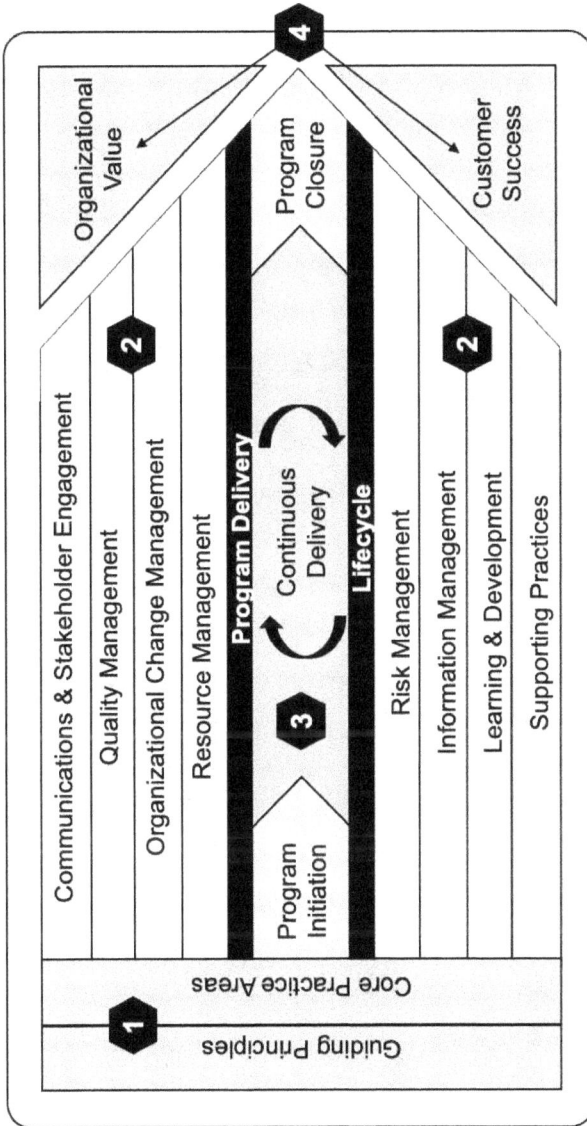

*Figure 10.* The Program Delivery Framework combines the need for governance and alignment, while providing delivery support resulting in a responsive and flexible structure that accommodates emerging changes while focusing on customer success.

The Program Management Practices are presented in the white sections above and below the Program Delivery Lifecycle in the framework above (denoted as #2). The practices are comprised of seven core and three supporting practices. In Part IV, each practices area includes a sub-section to discuss techniques to improve agility for that specific practice. The book shares techniques for agility that include responsiveness, competency, flexibility, speed, and stakeholder satisfaction for each of the program management practice areas.

The central portion of the framework (denoted as #3), Program Delivery Lifecycle, includes the work to startup a program, deliver the value intended, and close out the program once the program's purpose has been satisfied. This is presented in Part V. This area includes the practices (shown as #2) and discusses how and when they are applied throughout. In this area all the core practice areas and individual practices fuse together to govern, align, and support program delivery.

Finally, the two focus areas (on the far right, denoted as #4) stand as key measures for the program's success in the outcomes must provide value for both the performing organization and the customer who receives the value. Considering the continuous delivery of value, the outcomes and measurable value are also discussed in Part V along with the program delivery lifecycle. Before focusing on the program management practices, it is important to discuss the importance and influence of organizational strategy.

## The Role of Organizational Strategy

Strategy drives programs. An organizational strategy is the sum of the actions a company intends to take to achieve long-term goals (Johnson, 2019). The CEO and executive team play a big role in setting the foundation of a strategic plan by developing a strategic vision, creating guiding organizational principles, articulating the strategic areas of focus, and creating the long-term goals that guide the organization to create aligned goals and actions to achieve its vision of success (On Strategy, 2018). In business, the "North Star" represents a company's unwavering definition of its purpose, its products, its customers, and potential acquirers. Clarity about a company's North Star leads founders and companies toward their goals and helps investors envision the company's future growth (Shepard, 2022).

The lack of a North Star is also a primary reason for an organization's demise. In 2021, CB Insights conducted a study to determine the top 12 reasons for startup failure by analyzing 110+ startup organizations. The top five: ran out of cash/investments, no market need, flawed business model, got outcompeted, and regulatory challenges clearly point to a lack of strategy or customer knowledge and engagement. By understanding the market opportunities and ever-changing customer needs, an organization will better position itself for success.

Setting the right North Star is also an imperative to success. In January 2023, Toyota announced their current CEO, Akio Toyoda, will step down from his post. His departure was not unexpected given he has been a vocal skeptic of the global efforts to shift to battery-powered electric cars (Dooley, 2023). His successor, Koji Sato, has been a top executive at Toyota's luxury subsidiary, Lexus. He will be charged with two key strategic objectives: 1) To realign the company to meet the growing worldwide demand for electric vehicles and 2) Positioning Toyota to meet current and future mobility demands (e.g., Autonomous Vehicles, Micro-mobile vehicles, etc.) (Printz, 2023).

In the case above, the program should have the agility / flexibility to pivot its focus to new strategies as they are communicated. While program management teams do not set strategy, Strategic Alignment is a program management core practice area. Program teams align with strategies by building out and maintaining a roadmap to guide the teams throughout the program lifecycle. The program team then elicits organization, team, and customer inputs to continually refine and reprioritize the roadmap and program backlog. As a result of this work, the program team ensures delivery and operational activities are aligned and resources are best positioned and supported to deliver on the shared strategic vision. While delivering on strategy, program teams collect, summarize, and provide feedback to the Program Sponsor and Steering Committee members to potentially inform future organizational strategies.

# Chapter 10:

# Guiding Principles

Guiding Principles are used across the program life cycle to support both the coordination and achievement of team efforts and aid in decision-making throughout the lifecycle of the program. The Organizational Agility themes described earlier provide a basis for

> **Guiding Principles**
> "…as the strategy becomes clearer to more of the people in the company, it really makes things much easier…Simple can be harder than complex: You have to work hard to get your thinking clean to make it simple. But it's worth it in the end because once you get there, you can move mountains."
> – Steve Jobs
> (Andy Reinhardt, Business Week interview, May 24,1998)

techniques and guiding principles that can be applied to program management. Guiding principles should include a small set of heuristics (i.e., rules of thumb) to guide decision making at all levels.

One of my consulting opportunities included working with an Information Technology team within a hospitality organization. They were laser focused on their core guiding principle. I heard this in many meetings when deciding on a course of action for proposed changes, the number one consideration was on "the impact to the guest experience." This simple yet powerful approach provides clarity and is easy for everyone in the organization to understand and apply at all levels.

In order to provide a list of guiding principles that would suffice for many types of organizations, several guiding principles were reviewed from Program Management standards, books, and methods; Agile and Agile@Scale methods, practices, frameworks and toolsets (e.g., Disciplined Agile, Dynamic Systems Delivery Method [DSDM], Large Scale Scrum [LeSS], Scaled Agile Framework® [SAFe], Nexus Framework, Recipes for Agile Governance in the Enterprise ™ [RAGE], Scrum of Scrums [SoS], Scaling Agile @ Spotify [Spotify Model]); the Agile Manifesto and agile practices and frameworks (e.g., Scrum Guide, Kanban); and management theories, methods, and practices (including Fayol, Taylor, Weber, Von Bertalanffy, Burke and Litwin, Peters, and Deming). In this research, I found as few as three (i.e., Spotify) and as many as 14 guiding principles (or values, etc.) in some models. Three common guiding principles from the research above emerged that included:

- Focus on Customer Success.
- Foster a Culture of Respect.
- Create Organizational Value.

The three guiding principles defined above should be considered as a baseline for any additional guiding principles added. If an overarching principle is applied, the customer, team, and organization should always be considered when applying the guidance.

## The 5P Decision Support Matrix

As stated above, guiding principles serve as "golden rules" for organizations to aid in decision making. To answer the question regarding which guiding principles to apply to a certain organization, it is important to understand what is prioritized as most important to that organization. If the guidance above is not sufficient, one may consider applying principles developed by their organization, using those associated with the method currently in use, or a third option, using the *5P Decision Support Matrix* below.

I developed and applied the *5P Decision Support Matrix* (Figure 11) on many programs to aid in decision-making. I created this model, in part, because I couldn't remember 14 guiding principles, situations often called for more data to support the decisions, and this model provided me (and the team) with a simple method to aid in our decision making when posed with multiple seemingly viable alternatives or single go/no go type decisions.

| 5P Decision Support Matrix | | |
|---|---|---|
| | Present | Potential |
| People | √ | √ |
| Product | √ | √ |
| Process | √ | √ |

*Figure 11.* The 5P Decision Support Matrix includes practices areas that are performed throughout the lifecycle of a program.

To use the tool, the facilitator asks the team to consider the three factors on the left side and the two time horizons on the top, one at a time. Sub-factors are assessed for each major factor area. When considering options or next steps, what is the impact to people? This includes stakeholder groups that include customers, end users, team members, management, internal and external stakeholders. People are the first consideration due to the understanding that without the support of stakeholders, the other factors may not matter.

The second decision support factor is that of the product. If the first factor does not yield a single direction, then this second factor is considered. In all cases it is important to consider the time horizon factor. For example, if a new feature

> **Technical Debt**
> "Technical debt refers to the practice of relying on temporary easy-to-implement solutions to achieve short-term results at the expense of efficiency in the long run." (Tkachuk, 2021).
> The metaphor was coined by Ward Cunningham in 2009, co-author of Agile Manifesto, as a metaphor for describing the impact of accruing tech issues.

was selected and included today that would fundamentally limit the direction for the future, that could be a deciding factor in the selection of alternatives as this could create unwanted technical debt.

The third factor is that of the process. This considers the end-to-end process (or value chain) that the change impacts. Now that the people and product are well understood, the process could accelerate or limit the speed to market. Consider, for example, if the change introduces a new requirement for an additional approval or external step in a workflow. How would that impact the overall process? This may potentially yield a negative or a positive impact. The net is that it is important to understand and assess that impact before applying resources to the change activity.

In some organizations, some would specifically add a 6th P, representing Planet. This sustainability factor is considered in the other three, however, some may request it is called out specifically. Teams have found the matrix to provide a simple and collaborative method to elicit the inputs of the team, customers, and users and it helps build strong relationships within the team, customers, and other key stakeholders.

# Chapter 11:

# Program Governance

Program governance is a core practice area in the Program Delivery Framework and includes systems and methods by which a program is directed, evaluated, and monitored to ensure proper accountability,

> **Program Governance**
> Separating Governance from Management ensures an independent and accountable group or person provides oversight to ensure risks are appropriately managed, work is strategically aligned, and progress is proceeding as planned.

responsibility, awareness, impartiality, and transparency (Byrne, 2022). The primary objective of program governance is to ensure the investment in the program yields the desired outcomes that were either: (a) defined when the program was first chartered and/or, (b) continues to support the changing needs of the sponsoring organization throughout the life of the program.

The Program Manager ensures the program's delivery of business value is driven through a continuous review cycle to maintain alignment with the organization's strategic plan. Alignment, however, is only one indicator of potential value. Intervening factors relative to potential risks and issues must be considered.

For example, if a benefit is time bound (e.g., earlier delivery provides first mover advantage, resulting in implicit greater long-term revenue), and a risk to that time horizon is realized and becomes an issue, the net value may be reduced. Guidance for prioritizing value can be calculated using a Weighted Shortest Job First (WSJF) calculation to determine a calculated cost of a delay. Therefore prioritization, risk planning, and mitigation are core to value realization. To meet these goals, an accountability framework (e.g., Program Steering Committee, Program Management Office, etc.) and corresponding systems, processes, guidelines, and checkpoints must be established to periodically assess and adjust to address the current operating environment.

## Governance vs. Management

The terms governance and management are often misused interchangeably. The Information Systems Audit and Control Association (ISACA) developed a globally accepted framework for optimizing enterprise IT governance that is used for nearly 70% of information technology governance audits internationally (Radovanovic, Radojević, Lucic & Šarac, 2010). Their framework, Control Objectives for Information and Related Technologies (COBIT) 2019, provides guidance to differentiate governance from management in organizations. COBIT 2019 includes 40 governance and management objectives organized into five domains (one governance and four management). Figure 12 provides a view of the governance domain, its five objectives, and four management domains (Thomas, 2019).

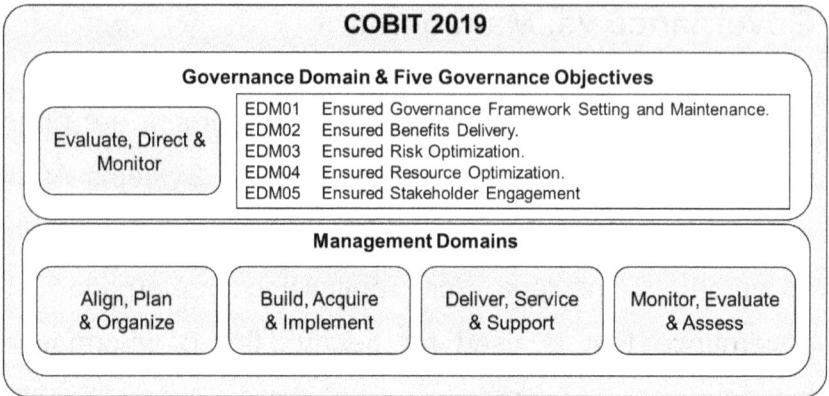

Figure 12. COBIT 2019 includes five domains and 40 objectives (five governance and 35 management) that meet a key COBIT principle to *separate governance from management* (Harisaiprasad, 2020).

Based on the model above, it becomes evident that the role of management is focused more on directly delivering value, whereas governance provides an oversight and delivery support function to oversee the alignment and delivery against the investment along that journey.

## Scope of Program Governance

As shown in Figure 13, a program's governance structure has two touchpoints: (1) between Portfolios and Programs and, (2) between a Program and associated Delivery and Operations Teams. The lines in the model below are perforated and non-linear to reflect the transparency of information flow as well as the joint negotiated accountability between and among the teams.

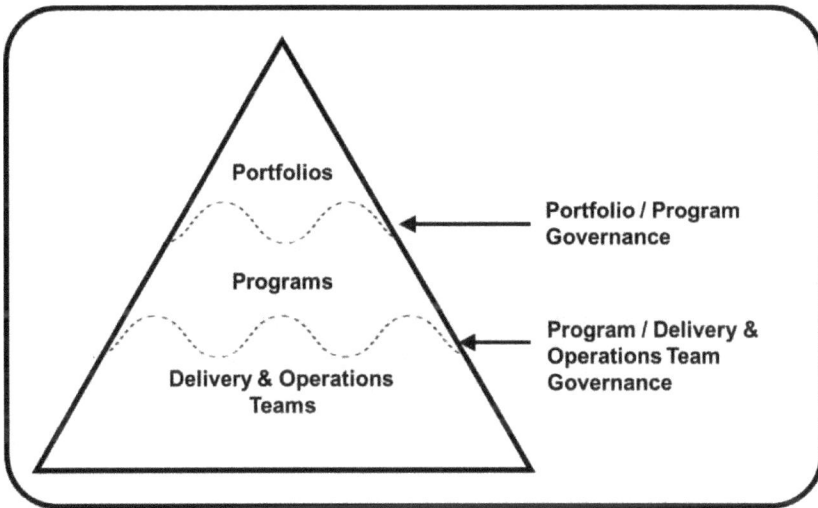

*Figure 13*. Programs are involved in governance at two levels: Portfolio/Program and Program/Delivery & Operations Teams.

Governance is more than simply holding meetings for oversight. Core governance components includes processes, organizational structures, information flows, policies, and applications. The goals of governance at each of the levels above are common and include:

- Ensuring the investments remain strategically aligned and effectively applied throughout the program lifecycle;
- Validating that decision-making is conducted at the appropriate level(s) to ensure transparency, visibility and alignment with the underlying business cases that initiated the activity;
- Reviewing the status against current priorities and redefining the direction if necessary;
- Assessing and mitigating risks/issues to ensure the program goals are met; and
- Allocating the appropriate resources across multiple programs and other activities to reflect the priorities and support the initiatives.

Governance at the levels shown above may differ in the organizational structure or level of information discussed. The following sections provide information relative to the differences found at the varying levels.

### *Portfolio/Program Governance*

Portfolio/Program governance is facilitated through a series of remote and in-person reviews, formal and informal interactions, and/or self-service facilities (e.g., Program Intranet, Management Dashboards, etc.). The core oversight and decision-making body providing governance for programs is often referred to as a Program Steering Committee. This group is chaired by Program Sponsor and the core committee members often include:

- Senior executive members of the impacted business and information technology areas;
- Representatives from the customer organization;
- Other stakeholders with significant interest or influence (e.g., Product Managers, Operations leads, etc.); and
- Other Organizational Sponsors with interest in the Program.

The Program Manager (and often the Chief Architect) is an invited guest to the board and is not a "voting" member – supporting the requirement *to separate governance from management*. The Program Manager's role is to present the state of the program as objectively as possible.

The board meets on a regular basis (usually monthly) to review status, discuss priorities and upcoming changes, assess major risks and issues and mitigation plans, and evaluate any major areas for decision-making. If items are presented for decision-making, the Program Manager is expected to present options, pros/cons, and recommendations.

### Program/Delivery Team Governance

Program/Delivery Team governance is facilitated like the discussion above. The Program Manager meets with members of the change activities (products, projects, organizational change activities, services, solutions, other activities) on a periodic basis, usually every week but may differ based on the needs of the organization and methods chosen, in a variety of forums. The forums may include attending existing meetings that are led by the delivery teams, program coordination meetings hosted by the Program team (e.g., Program Team Meetings, Scrum of Scrums, Release Train Meetings, Architectural Review Boards, etc.) or one-on-one meetings with team leads. Meetings for significant events related to handover between organizations must include the appropriate stakeholders and many culminate in a formal "signoff" or documented agreement of the ongoing stewardship of the changes being deployed. The meeting agendas are varied but the focus on program-level risks, issues, priorities, current state, resources, and decisions of significant impact or any other pertinent business.

Self-service information is facilitated by the teams maintaining plan information in an Application Lifecycle Management (ALM), Enterprise Agile Planning (EAP) application or other repositories that can be mined to present summary information on management dashboards and/or Program Intranet sites.

## Program Governance Processes

Good governance practices help organizations build an environment of trust, transparency and accountability that support the investments in the change activities.

Separating Governance from Management ensures an independent and accountable group or person (e.g., Program Sponsor) provides oversight to ensure risks are appropriately managed, work is strategically aligned, and progress is proceeding as planned. There are many activities that take place when a program is first chartered to position it for success. These practices are discussed in Part IV and include:

- Identifying the stakeholders and communications events required for each level of governance (Chapter 13: Communications and Stakeholder Engagement);
- Defining Quality oversight procedures (Chapter 14 Quality Management);
- Preparing for Organizational Change (Chapter 15 Organizational Change Management);
- Gathering and allocating resources (e.g., financial, facilities, human, material, technology, etc.) (Chapter 16 Resource Management);
- Identifying and performing mitigation planning for potential risks and issues (Chapter 17 Risk Issue Management);

- Developing processes and procedures to manage and share program related information (Chapter 18 Information Management); and
- Preparing the teams for current and future challenges (Chapter 19 Learning & Development).

Additional "Supporting Practices" that are emerging and have gained significant attention and adoption are included in Part IV. Program governance related to the prioritization, selection, and authorization of work is discussed in Part V, Project Delivery Lifecycle & Outcomes. Specific processes are discussed in each respective chapter in that section.

## Techniques for Agility in Program Governance

The primary organizational agility theme associated with program governance is *structural flexibility*. Program (and organizational) governance must support internal structures and promote a culture that enables resources (e.g., financial, facilities, human, material, technology, etc.) to be easily applied as changes emerge. It must also allow for the seamless redirection of the resources based on changes in priorities. Techniques that support these requirements are detailed below.

### *Practice Lean Governance*

To provide agility in program management governance the team must place an emphasis on decentralized decision-making, streamlined processes, and standardized workflows. Complex governance and approval processes are the biggest barriers to speed (Planview, 2021). By assessing and implementing continuous improvement activities while implementing quality checkpoints, the program team can help increase speed and agility, and lower overall risks. Lean governance focuses on delivering value to the customer and ensuring that the right things are being done, rather than prescribing how they should be done. Using this mindset (sharing the intent, vs. the task steps) empowers the teams and yields the appropriate oversight without micromanagement.

### Decentralize decision-making – provide guardrails.

Some decisions, specifically those related to organizational strategy, should be centralized. Many others can be decentralized or shared based on the needs of the performing organization. For example, the prioritization of a User Story may be determined by a Product Owner, however, the assignment of specific delivery support tasks within a feature are decentralized to the team. A matrix of decision types and guardrails (upper/lower control limits) can be documented to provide clarity.

## Use data to inform decisions.

Data driven decision making is defined as using facts, metrics, and data to *guide* strategic business decisions that align with your goals, objectives, and initiatives (Tableau, 2022). The key word in this statement is *guide*. It is important for those involved in decision-making to use their experience and discretion to determine the best path forward with available data as an input to that end. There are times where data is unavailable and the effort to create it may significantly delay a decision. It should not become a roadblock. This is the time to rely on experience and discretion and move forward while assessing risks as appropriate.

## **Streamline approval processes and workflows.**

By simplifying or eliminating unnecessary approvals or work-related tasks, organizations will improve the efficiency of governance processes. Despite changes in methods, approvals often go through multiple levels of the organization because "we've always done it that way." Workflows should be periodically assessed to improve flow, remove unneeded steps/approvals, and reduce wait times. Kaizen events can be held to review and scrutinize the processes so that mistakes and waste can be minimized.

### *Agile Governance Sets a Foundation for Success*

By applying lean governance techniques and focusing on what really matters, delivery of outcomes, the program will position itself as capable and trustworthy. To support this capability, an understanding of organizational culture and the value of professional relationships cannot be ignored. While providing quick wins and taking proper measurements, the program can demonstrate its value early on and set the pace for future success.

## *Governance Impacts Culture*

Can agility and governance co-exist? It's a question many business and IT leaders struggle with as they implement Agile@Scale and as they work to improve governance processes. Program Steering Committees and Program Management Offices (PMO) alike strive to balance responsiveness with an increasing rate of change in business requests while maintaining some semblance of control to ensure quality outcomes are delivered. Vejseli, Rossmann & Garidis (2022) found that "agility must be viewed as a crucial concept for IT Governance" and "firms need to develop a basic governance model powered by traditional IT Governance mechanisms and mutually increase agility in their structures, processes, and relational mechanisms (p. 12)."

With this said, the right culture, controls, and supporting processes in place, it is possible for agility and governance to coexist while avoiding a command-and-control governance approach that slows delivery.

Throughout the program, consider the policies, processes, and procedures the program levies on the delivery teams. When emplacing controls, consider the downstream and cultural impacts of those controls. By employing Organizational Change Management techniques like co-creation, having delivery team involvement may: 1) streamline the change and lessen the impact to delivery teams and 2) Provide buy in and "compliance" by having the teams understand and share the purpose of the new requirements.

## **Professional relationships mean everything.**

Building good work relationships can have a huge impact on how much *you enjoy your job*. If you have solid relationships with your team and management, you'll be excited to go to work. You'll love the feeling of efficiency that comes with great teamwork. Anyone who's worked in a toxic workplace knows why good work relationships are important. Good professional relationships promote trust, mutual respect, collaborative decision-making, and honest and open communication (Waters, 2022).

These factors not only improve productivity but also make it easier when tough times come about. If you are a Program Manager and have a solid professional relationship with your manager, when problems arise, they may be more apt to support you and collaborate to come up with solutions than go in a different direction (i.e., possibly a Performance Improvement Plan) if you didn't have that same professional relationship.

## Focus on quick wins.

At the program initiation stage, the program start up activities gain a lot of attention because it sets the baseline to support delivery. It is important to remember that quick wins at startup are also important. Showing the ability to deliver early and often creates a "can-do" culture. While program startup activities are topical at the onset of a program, the intent of the investment is to deliver. It is important to maintain that focus and reflect it in the measurements and status reporting to ensure that the team is hyper focused on what truly matters.

## Measure what matters.

It is important to note, as the program matures different measures will become more pertinent and others will fall by the wayside. For example, in the beginning of a program efforts may be focused on two important aspects, quick wins and setting up the program for success. Program startup measures like number/percent of Non-disclosure Agreements and contracts signed quickly become replaced with metrics related to the delivery of change activities that provide business value. This does not mean that the former measures are incorrect. However, they may be relevant only during a limited time, such as the startup phase, and may not be tracked as closely as the program matures. The phrase "measure what matters" must take into account the program's time horizon and maturity. These measures should be periodically reviewed and updated to facilitate decision-making and guide appropriate actions and activities by the program team.

# Chapter 12:

# Program Strategic Alignment

It is imperative that the efforts of the programs and delivery teams consistently align with organizational strategy to achieve the goals defined in the strategic planning process. This core practice includes the processes to

> **Program Strategic Alignment**
> Includes the efforts to ensure change activities consistently align with the organizational strategies at both program initiation and throughout the continuous delivery lifecycle.

identify, define, track, realize, optimize, and sustain the benefits an organization realizes through change activities.

Throughout the process, there are checks and balances at the portfolio, program, and team levels to ensure the organization's investments are continuously aligned with and meeting the goals defined in the strategic plan. In the Strategic Planning process, the organization defines strategies, objectives, and measures of performance based on several factors. They may use a Balanced Scorecard approach to ensure the goals support need in four key domains that include: Financial, Customer, Internal Business Process and Learning and Growth perspectives (Kaplan & Norton, 2000).

The Portfolio Management teams responsible for each allocated strategy (e.g., HR Portfolio team for Learning and Development strategies) then determine the best way to break down this work into *initiatives* to achieve these objectives. The initiatives may take form as new programs, expanded scope to existing programs, individual projects, operational activities, or other change activities.

Benefits Management (aka benefits realization) is often discussed as a separate discipline. In the redefined model presented in this book, this is not a separate discipline, but integrated with strategic alignment. After all, what is being strategically aligned are in fact the intended organizational benefits. A benefit is an outcome that is not necessarily a new or improved product or service. For example, a valuable organizational benefit because of a change activity may be a change that "enabled our ability to shorten approval time for underwriting, yielding in a 25% reduction in cycle time, resulting in fewer calls from those seeking coverage and new Net Promoter Scores up 10% indicating overall improved customer satisfaction. This should allow us to increase market share by 5% in the next fiscal year."

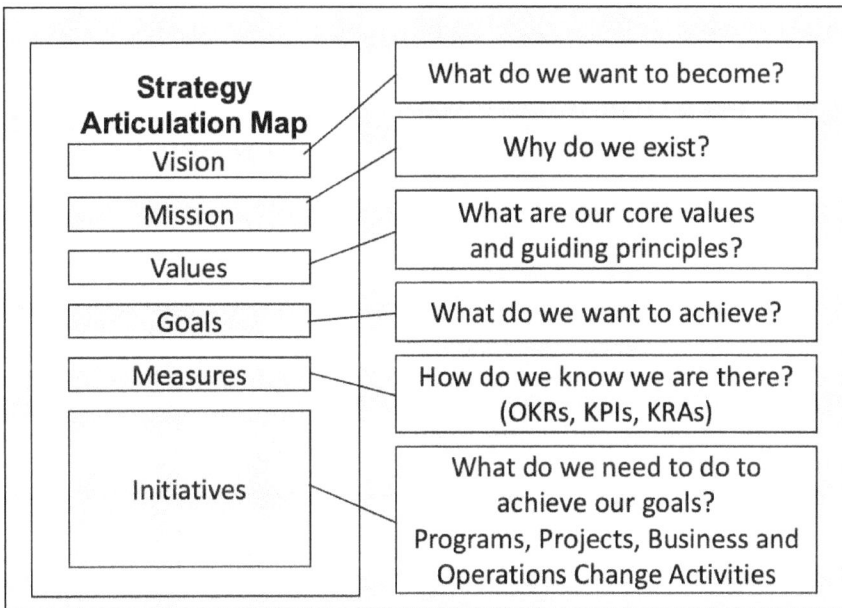

*Figure 14.* A Strategy Articulation Map helps communicate the organization's strategy on a single page.

An output from the strategic planning process (performed at the portfolio level) may include a formal strategic plan, strategy map, strategy canvas, strategy articulation map (see Figure 14), or other artifact that breaks down the updated (usually annual) strategy into an updated mission/vision statement and specific goals, measures, and initiatives to achieve those strategies in that period. Business cases are often developed for each initiative or group of initiatives, and then the appropriate teams are assigned to perform this work.

## Scope of Program Strategic Alignment

Following the definition of the initiatives for the upcoming period (usually annually), business cases are developed for those major initiatives identified. A business case is a work product that provides the justification for investing in that specific initiative. The

> **Business Case**
> Provides the justification for the investment in a change activity. It often includes the requested budget, justification, objectives, strategic contribution, achievability assessment, key deliverables, risks, resource requirements, impact on organization, and cost benefits analysis.
> *(Harrin, 2013)*

Portfolio team identifies the appropriate Sponsor for that effort, and the assigned sponsor (or their team) create the Business Case. In many cases, however, they may request support from an existing program team to write the business case and shepherd it through the approval process. As depicted in Figure 9, not all initiatives will become new programs, some will be delivered via a specific project, others may be assigned to an operations or business team, while others will be added to the scope of an existing program.

The program team is positioned between the portfolio team and the delivery teams (see Figure 15). Considering this arrangement, the program team needs to ensure they maintain bidirectional alignment with all involved entities. In support of this effort, the tasks of workflow management via multiple forums take place.

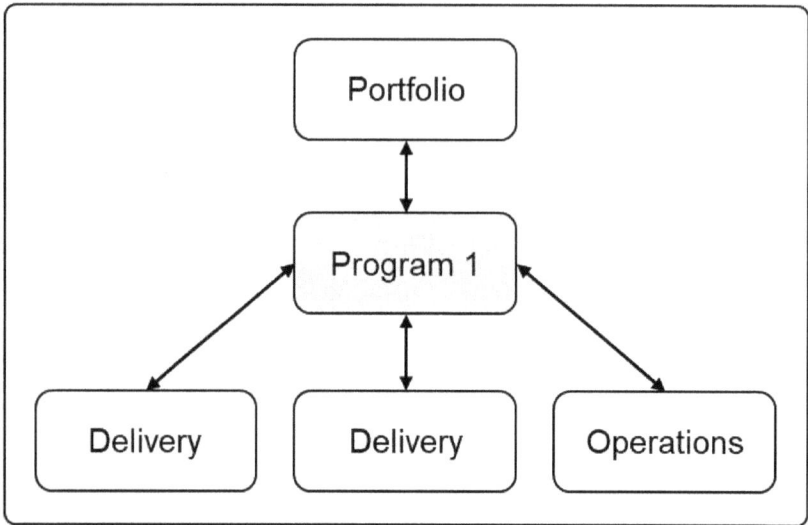

*Figure 15.* Program Management aligns bidirectionally with the portfolio, delivery, and operations teams.

## Strategic Alignment Process

Once the business case is approved, the Sponsor will select a Program Manager (or another team lead) to manage the delivery of the work. If the initiative is assigned to a program, a Program Charter and Program Roadmap are developed to describe the plans for that program. For cases where a program team is already established, that new scope of work will be combined and reprioritized along with the current scope of work and the artifacts are updated as appropriate.

The Program Charter in the past was a *document* that provided a concise description of the program justification, vision, governance, alignment, benefits, scope, assumptions/constraints, risks/issues, goals objectives, critical success factors, stakeholders, and timing (overall schedule). Today, since most programs have an intranet page, it is often more efficient to place the appropriate information in this medium to communicate this same information. Much of the information for the charter can be copied from the business case. Depending on the sensitivity of work involved, Program Managers need to use discretion in terms of the information provided in this forum. The Charter is still a good work product for communications if the size of the effort justifies it. Often there is a lag between when a business case is approved, and the charter is written. During this period ambiguity can creep in regarding the intent of the initiative. A charter can be an effective work product to realign the stakeholders prior to beginning a significant new effort.

Following the development of the program charter, an initial program roadmap is developed. The roadmap provides a high-level *forecast* of when significant portions of the overall scope may be delivered. Since the work in programs is frequently reprioritized, this *forecast* should be updated as appropriate when major changes occur. As a part of this process, interdependencies between change activities are identified and interrogated to determine any potential impact. These interdependencies commonly take form of predecessor or successor relationships among program change activities. This means if a change activity must be completed before another starts, it will have an impact on the delivery of the successor activity. This could change the priority of the predecessor activity if the successor was deemed initially of a higher priority considering the predecessor must now complete first and therefore becomes the priority (or critical path) to achieve the formerly higher priority successor activity.

Other types of interdependent activities must be considered if the culmination of several change activities will subsume or replace a current product, service, process, etc. This may cause all related change activities to complete before the result is deliverable/consumable.

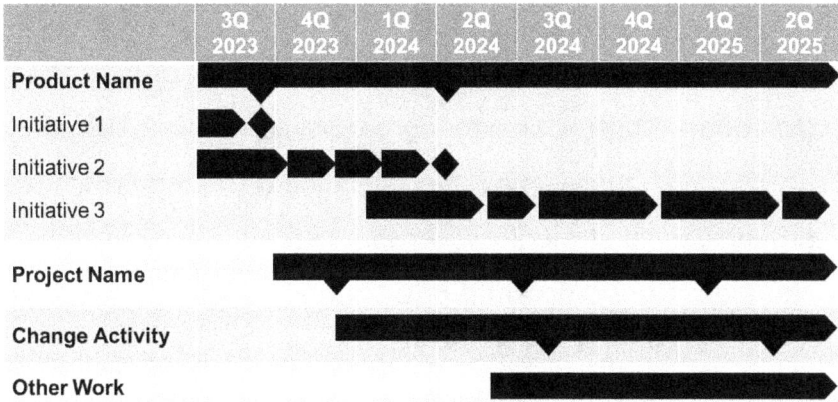

*Figure 16.* A Program Roadmap provides a high-level view of the work planned for the program.

The program roadmap may be presented as a Gantt chart (as above) or depicted as a graphical chart with milestones and high-level capabilities plotted on a timeline. An important note is that the roadmap is a *forecast* that represents the information known at a given time and *will likely change* in response to changes at the portfolio level, changes in the operating environment, customer requested changes, and/or other changes due to management discretion.

The Program management team then "initiates, defines, redefines, accelerates, or terminates change activities in a program in accordance with achieving the overall strategic goals and vision of that organization" (Naybour, 2020). Considering programs may run for years at a time, there may be significant changes to the organizational strategies over that same time necessitating changes in the program. For example, if a group of change activities within a program was initially desired and later, due to technological changes, deemed ineffective, that portion of the program could be halted, and the resources may be applied to the integration of the newer technology.

Following the initial alignment as work is defined to support the organizational strategies, several ongoing activities are performed to maintain the alignment.

Portfolio to Program alignment activities may include periodic:

- Portfolio oversight meetings (Status, Risk, and Budget Reviews)
- Program Steering Committee
- Program Sponsor/Product Manager meetings
- Roadmap meetings (e.g., Roadmap Reviews, Program Increment (SAFe), etc.)

<u>Program to Delivery team alignment</u> activities may include:

- Program Delivery Coordination Meetings
- Product Owner meetings
- Prototypes and Demos
- Project Meetings/Scrum Ceremonies

Program Delivery Coordination Meetings (aka Scrum of Scrums [SoS]) are central to Strategic Alignment. Depending upon the size and complexity of the program the Program Manager themselves may facilitate the delivery coordination meetings or identify a Program Delivery Manager to facilitate meetings. This is not a status meeting but facilitated interactions between and among teams intended to assess new opportunities, validate priorities of upcoming change activities, coordinate cross team efforts, remove roadblocks, align organizational outputs, and record benefits achieved. This meeting may occur daily, bi-weekly, or weekly depending upon the needs of the teams. A typical agenda might include (Agile Alliance, 2023; Murray, 2023):

- Review of previous meeting notes and action items;
- Updates from each representative on their respective team's progress;
- Discussion of cross-team dependencies and any blockers that need to be addressed;
- Review of upcoming sprint plans and coordination between teams;
- Identification and discussion of any cross-team risks or challenges; and
- Any other business that needs to be addressed.

The agenda should be flexible enough to allow for discussion and problem-solving, but also structured enough to ensure that important topics are covered. The facilitators should ensure action items are identified, assigned, and subsequently closed.

The corresponding Agile@Scale roles and methods may include Senior Scrum Master (e.g., Scrum of Scrums, Disciplined Agile® Delivery, others), Tribe Lead (i.e., Spotify), Release Train Engineer (i.e., SAFe), Scrum Master, Service Delivery Manager (SDM), Service Request Manager (SRM), or Iteration Manager (i.e., Enterprise

Kanban) or other title depending upon the individual or mix of delivery methods used in the performing organization.

In addition to the communications events described above, program internet sites with embedded "dashboards" should be in place so at any time the stakeholders may have (role-based) self-service access to real time (or near real time) program information. Role-based access is important depending on the data being shared. Not all team members have a need to know all things about the program.

By setting up the program to align with the organization's strategies, and putting in place the appropriate governance structures, the program should always be positioned to quickly sense and efficiently respond to changes in the environment.

## Techniques for Agility in Strategic Alignment

The ability to sense and respond to opportunities and changes in the environment is a core tenant of organizational agility. To be a first mover or fast follower can make the difference between those organizations that thrive and those that merely survive (and possibly not for long). Maintaining strategic alignment in programs and throughout the organization brings stakeholder satisfaction to the forefront. This practice area most closely aligns with the organizational agility theme of *strategic alignment and responsiveness.*

**Explore Opportunities for Responsiveness**

Opportunities for program responsiveness can be found in the processes the program follows and in the change activities the program produces or enables. There is often a fine line between responsive and reactionary. The program team certainly wants to be viewed as former and must put in place a framework and processes to support this need. Reactionary organizations often lack plans or processes to deal with uncertainty or environmental changes.

**Select Common Delivery Frameworks**

During program startup, teams are assembled. As work begins, the teams select a delivery framework that supports their needs. It is important to 1) Select a common framework so training is minimized, and the team can begin quickly, while 2) Selecting the appropriate framework for the work under consideration. If the team is familiar with waterfall, and the work is complex software development, the investment in training in an Agile or Agile@Scale method may prove beneficial even if the initial startup takes a bit longer than using the framework those are familiar with rather than following an inappropriate method for the work at hand.

Using a standardized framework enables responsiveness as program management processes and practices can be defined alongside the framework to support the appropriate response to change requests.

## Set Prioritization Processes

Responsive is not equal to reactive. Reactive is often related with not having a plan or process to handle uncertainty or environmental changes. It can be difficult when presented with an "emergency" change and not react to it – especially if it is presented by someone at a level higher than yourself in the organization. It's at this point that it becomes important to leverage processes to define the highest priority, keeping in mind that management discretion can override all other inputs.

When presented with a high priority or emergency change, the program team should research against current work. Following this assessment, they should vet this change with the program sponsor (and possibly the product manager/owner). If it is indeed deemed an emergency, then the team should flex to focus on this new priority. The assessment process should be lean, so the process takes only a few hours at most. Delaying emergency changes due to inefficient processes can pose significant costs to organizations.

## Create a Forum for Ideation

Provide a forum (e.g., virtual whiteboard, preliminary backlog, etc.) for new ideas so they may be captured in real-time. Brainstorming events may be conducted periodically to assess new possibilities or solutions to meet the current and future program objectives. It is helpful to provide an ideation or demand management application to collect information, vote on, justify, and select proposed change activities as they are presented. As each is assessed, the requester or a solution architect can document the cost and benefits in support of the selection of the new opportunity.

## Continually Assess Alignment

In order to achieve strategic alignment, processes and checkpoints must be emplaced to assess, review and if needed, redirect the program or specific change activities. While there are many meetings within a program and the delivery teams, it is important to identify those opportunities that provide the most value to assess the current state without disrupting the flow.

## **Continually Review Priorities**

Not every change is an emergency change. If every change is treated as an emergency, it may indicate a cultural problem. When new changes are presented, they should be evaluated objectively, just like any other change request. This means considering the overall strategy and prioritizing based on its importance. By conducting an analysis of the relative value of new and existing initiatives, it's possible to ensure that all projects are properly prioritized. It's crucial to address this issue early on in the process to prevent unnecessary stress and disruption. New work should be assessed as all other work is assessed. If the overall strategy has changed and it is indeed deemed more important, that will be determined via this vetting and analysis process.

## Take a 360-Degree View

While the portfolio maintains alignment amongst programs under its umbrella, it is also important for Program Managers to understand other programs that may be providing complementary outcomes so that they balance and align, rather than duplicate efforts. While reviewing the work within the current program, information about complementary or duplicative efforts may arise. It is important to determine if there are synergies that can be leveraged or if there are truly duplicative efforts occurring. As an example, if a group of servers are moving to the cloud, it is helpful to understand if any other work is planned for these same servers (e.g., upgrades, replacements, etc.). By understanding the impact, there may be an opportunity to save the organization the cost of work that may be wasted if performed.

## Question the Status Quo of In-Progress Work

If you're working on something and nobody is asking for updates, it's worth questioning whether it's still considered valuable. On the other hand, if you're getting many requests for something, it's worth considering whether it objectively has a higher priority. The squeaky wheel should only get the grease when objectivity is applied. We often see work that continues to be developed despite changes in the environment that would suggest that change may no longer be required.

# Part IV: Program Delivery Support Practices

# Part IV:

# Program Delivery Support

# Practices

Program Delivery Support Practices include *foundational* practices that are required on most programs to achieve the desired organizational benefits while applying the principles of organizational agility. The delivery practices described in this section complete the three core practice areas of Governance, Strategic Alignment and Delivery Support that have been used throughout this book. The effective and efficient application of the core practices described in this Chapter can significantly enhance the potential for program success while the absence often results in major impediments.

A primary responsibility of the program team is to align the delivery teams with the organization's goals and support them by maintaining stakeholder communications back to

> **Agile Principle**
> "The most efficient and effective method of conveying information to and within a development team is face-to-face conversation."
> (Fowler & Highsmith, 2001)

the portfolio teams, providing alignment across the organization, and governance and delivery support within and across each delivery team to facilitate the successful achievement of the program's outcomes.

The program environment, depicted below in Figure 17, shows a collaborative organizational structure with many entities that need to be coordinated to achieve organizational strategic goals. At the center of the diagram, the program team serves as an intermediary between teams to aid in the coordinated delivery of organizational benefits.

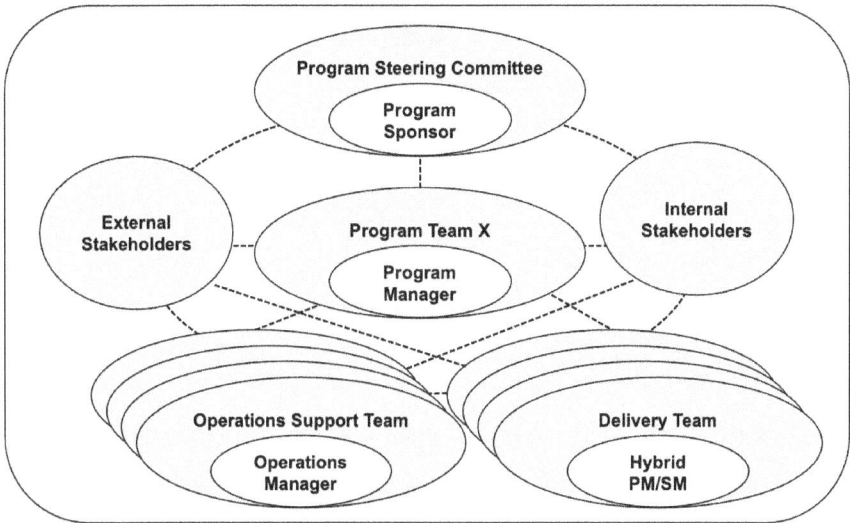

*Figure 17*. Program teams help organizations achieve their goals through the collaborative and coordinated practices within their purview.

To provide this requisite value, the program team performs several functions that include:

- Communications and Stakeholder Engagement
- Quality Management
- Organizational Change Management
- Risk/Issue Management
- Resource Management
- Information Management

- Learning and Development
- Supporting Practices

Absent from this book are those practices that are either primarily "project" oriented (i.e., schedule and scope management are primarily project practices, programs focus on a different level of scope [e.g., roadmaps]) and/or practice areas that have been either subsumed by others (e.g., benefits management is an integral part of strategic alignment) or practices are now considered archaic (e.g., communications vehicles [e.g., documents vs. intranet sites]).

One other key artifact that will not be found in this book is a Program Management Plan. This monolithic artifact has failed to prove its value as a standalone work product. The processes commonly found in this document (vice those specifically excluded above) should continue but in a lightweight format. These remaining practices are discussed throughout Part IV.

# Chapter 13:

# Communications and Stakeholder Engagement

Program communications and stakeholder engagement practices are the cornerstone of program delivery support. Considering the complexity and impact

<table>
<tr><td>Stakeholders<br>Include internal and external individuals, groups, or organizations who have an interest in the program who may directly or indirectly, positively, or negatively impact the program outcomes.</td></tr>
</table>

programs have on organizational benefits, it is imperative to successfully communicate and engage stakeholders with the right message at the right time. Delays in communications can have significant rippling impacts. These practices support the program by ensuring the appropriate stakeholder communities are identified, assessed, and engaged to achieve the desired program outcomes. A single stakeholder can have a significant impact on the program resulting in delays, scope changes or decommissioning of the program. It is important to recognize who the stakeholders are and to understand their power and influence to engage them properly to minimize any potential risks.

## Scope of Program Communications

At the beginning of the program a Program Communications and Stakeholder Engagement plan is developed. This plan is used to identify the stakeholder communities impacted, determine the appropriate communications, methods, and frequency for engaging specific stakeholders. The plan then lists those responsible for maintaining specific communications at the program or delivery team. The plan is updated as delivery teams are established and again periodically to reflect changes in stakeholders.

When developing a program communications plan, it is important to decide which communications will be managed by the program, and which will be managed by the delivery teams. The delivery team may leverage the program communications plan or develop their own "team-level" communication plan. Program communications generally involve a stakeholder community whose interests and needs span across multiple change activities within a program.

For example, the Program Sponsor, business/IT executives and/or senior management may need to understand the state of the overall program at a summary level. The program management team is responsible for this type of communication. If the Product Owner has a need to understand the timing of the delivery of new features, they would generally work with the delivery team responsible for that change activity considering they work with them on a frequent basis. However, they may need to refer to a program roadmap to see across future forecasts of planned work at the program level.

## Communications Process

The Communications process is comprised of three general steps: identification, assessment, and engagement. As described above, the outcome of the above activities is documented in a Communications and Stakeholder Engagement Plan. Once developed, the plan is frequently updated to reflect changes in program team members and stakeholders and in response to the evolving needs of the stakeholder communities, individual stakeholders, or the program itself.

## Stakeholder Identification

The identification of the stakeholder communities is the first step. Stakeholders include internal and external individuals, groups, or organizations who have an interest in the program who may directly or indirectly, positively, or negatively impact the program outcomes. I developed an acronym to aid in the identification of stakeholders. At the beginning and throughout a program, the program delivery team needs to "listen to the *MUSIC*." MUSIC being an acronym for the following categories of stakeholders:

- Members (of the performing organization): Program sponsors, management (Executives and Senior management), Business Owners, Product Managers, Lead Architects, program steering committee, delivery team members, operations team members, supporting teams (Legal, Contracts, Procurement, Security, etc.) and other internal stakeholders.

- User Community: Includes those who directly use the product, service, process, or outcome from the program or those who represent the user community. Internal/external, current/potential customers, integrators, unions, trade organizations, etc. are included in this category.

- Suppliers: Business partners may include suppliers providing products or components, vendors providing value added services to the program, contractors providing expertise, or organizations that have agreed to joint ventures/go-to-market alliances.

- Influencers: Research organizations (Better Business Bureau (BBB), Forrester, Gartner, International Data Corporation (IDC), Nielsen, etc.), internet communities of interest (COINS) (e.g., LinkedIn Groups, etc.), Government or government lobby groups, local and national media, social media, search engine optimization (SEO), and other marketing influencers (Facebook Ads, etc.) must be considered for both potential positive and negative impacts.

- Competitors: It is important to understand industry trends and offerings by your direct and indirect competitors. Knowing what your competitors are doing provides an opportunity to create value for your existing customers and/or this knowledge can provide the potential to attract new customers.

While the categories above a presented separately, there are many occasions where an individual, group or organization will fall within more than one of these categories. For example, if using a subcontractor for staff augmentation, these resources may be considered as part of the *members* category (vs. suppliers). When identifying stakeholders, it's important to consider both internal and external stakeholders. The categories are initially entered in a table and the team comes together to brainstorm the names of the individuals, groups or organizations of stakeholders falling within each *MUSIC* category.

## Stakeholder Assessment

Once the stakeholders are identified, an assessment is required to level of communications and outreach based on the power/ interest of the stakeholders. Aubrey Mendelow (1991) published the Power-Interest

Matrix (see Figure 18) to help identify the communications needs of stakeholders within and external to the performing organization.

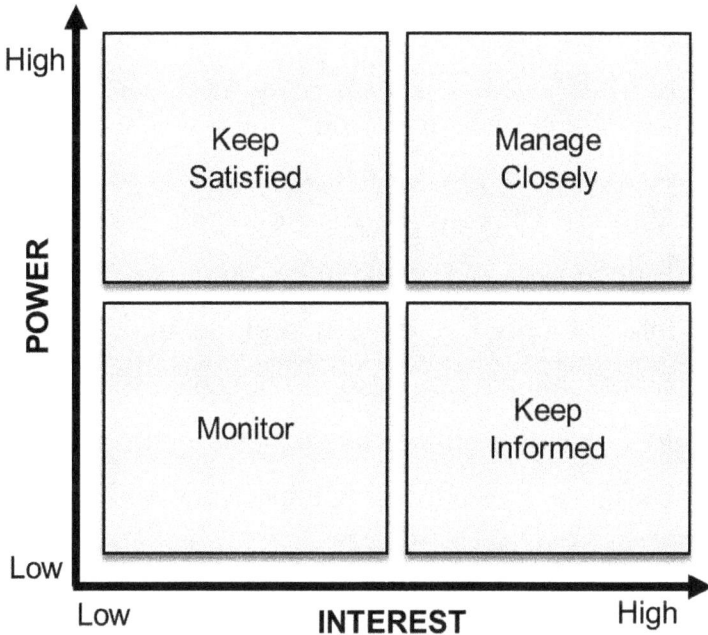

*Figure 18.* The Power/Interest Matrix (Eden & Ackerman,1998) describes interactions required based on stakeholder types. Reprinted with permission.

The matrix includes quadrants that describe the type of interaction to facilitate with stakeholders based on their relative power to the program and their implied relative level of interest in initiative. The power and interest are initially based on their professional role more so than their personal affinities. As management approaches differ over time, the types of communications and interactions will also change to suit the individual needs as appropriate. The different approaches include:

- **Manage Closely:** The stakeholders that fall in the High power – High interest area are likely to be internal decision makers and generally have the greatest impact on program success. It is important to regularly engage and consult with those in this category to best manage their expectations.

- **Keep satisfied:** Stakeholders with High power – Low Interest need to be informed and engaged in the program, but at a different level than those in the previous category. It is important to understand that while the interest may be lower, the power is still high and they could use their power in either a positive or negative manner, helping or hindering program success. Some in this category can be accommodated by providing a link to the program webpage while others may require a periodic check in (meeting or email) to gauge their needs.

- **Keep Informed:** Low power – High interest stakeholders need to be kept adequately informed to verify there are no unknown issues arising. This two-way interaction is used to both share and garner information.

- **Monitor:** Stakeholders with Low power – Low interest are those who either the program team shares basic information with or seeks information from. This category is the lowest "touch" group, but the understanding of their needs and actions may help inform the program direction. For example, if a competitor falls in this category, it's important to know what unique value they are offering for consideration for your current program.

To map out stakeholders across the quadrants, I developed The Communication Alignment Matrix to quickly associate program communications with stakeholder's needs. Figure 19 shows three groups of stakeholders based on the *MUSIC* acronym presented earlier.

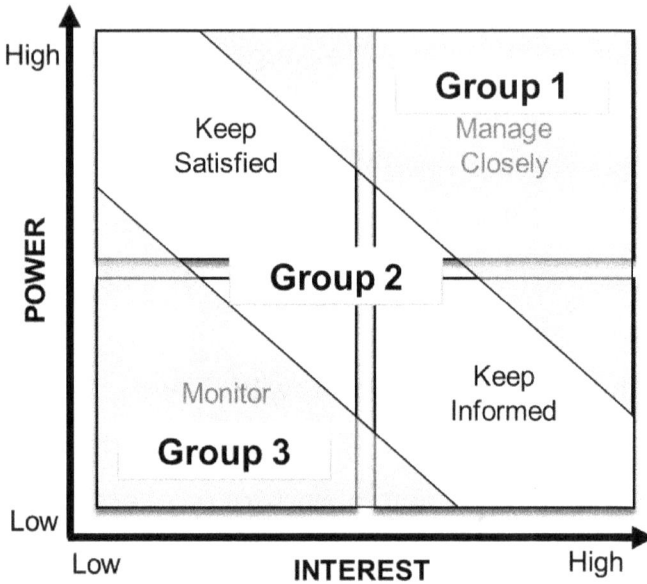

*Figure 19.* The Communications Alignment Matrix is used to accelerate the mapping of stakeholders to the Power/Influence Matrix to quickly define the type of interactions required based on the needs of the program and of the groups of stakeholders. Adapted with permission.

The stakeholder names, groups, or organizations identified earlier are placed in the matrix above generally as follows:

- Group 1: Includes Members and User Community.
- Group 2: Includes Suppliers and Influencers.
- Group 3 includes Competitors.

Once the initial mapping is completed using the Communications Alignment Matrix, the program team can then refine the stakeholder list based on those with more or fewer needs. As stated earlier, over time, those in the High/High quadrant can be reassessed based on their individual needs.

## Stakeholder Engagement

The final step in the process is to develop a communications plan. The plan is used to define the messages, channels, frequency, and stakeholders for each communications event. The result is plotted in a communications plan (see Figure 20) and periodically updated based on changes in stakeholders or changes in their needs.

| Program Communications Plan | | | | | | |
|---|---|---|---|---|---|---|
| Stakeholder | Message | Media | Frequency | Timing | Responsible | Notes |
| | | | | | | |
| | | | | | | |
| | | | | | | |
| | | | | | | |

*Figure 20.* The Communications Plan is used to define the events used to inform, share, or gather information from stakeholders.

In the plan above, the program team first adds the stakeholders identified earlier and then discusses how to best meet the needs of the individuals, groups or organizations based on the required messaging. The fields include:

- Stakeholders: List all stakeholders from the MUSIC categories.
- Message: Define the information that is planned to be disseminated or gathered via the communications event.
- Media/Vehicle: May include direct interactions (meetings, email, open office hours, training, etc.) or

indirect interactions (program webpage, dashboards, newsletters, blogs, internal/external social media, etc.).

- <u>Frequency</u>: Daily, Weekly, Bi-Monthly, Monthly, Ad Hoc, etc. This could also be tied to the start or completion of a program activity (for example: at a completion milestone).

- <u>Timing</u>: If monthly, this may be the 3$^{rd}$ Tuesday of each month. If weekly, this may be Tuesday at 10:00 AM (be sure to indicate the time zone).

- <u>Responsible</u>: This is the person who prepares for and facilitates the event.

- <u>Notes</u>: Just because there is always something that the other categories miss. This could include: The Sponsor has all day meetings on Mondays, do not schedule at that time. Or other notes.

The plan is updated frequently to reflect ongoing changes to both the stakeholders involved and the changing needs of this community. When considering competitors, remember to include them on the plan, even if this is a quarterly research event to identify any new feature or direction in that they are taking their product.

## Techniques for Agility in Communications

Through the process of identification, assessment and stakeholder engagement, there may be many opportunities to improve agility. This practice area most closely aligns with the organizational agility theme of *market and stakeholder understanding*. Below are some techniques for consideration.

### *Optimize Communications Forums*

Your stakeholder's scarcest resource is time (Mankins, Brahm & Caimi, 2014). There are many best practices for optimizing people's time as it relates to communications. By selecting the appropriate communications type, providing self-service opportunities for stakeholders to access information relevant to their needs, and limiting and applying best practices for "face-to-face" type meetings, this will maximize the time for all impacted stakeholders' resulting in better communications and overall satisfaction for both customers and team members alike.

## Use a Stakeholder Map

Using the Initial Stakeholder Map (provided earlier in this Chapter) to chart out Stakeholder needs can help provide the right information at the right time. There are multiple ways to gather information relative to the stakeholder community your program engages. When possible, consider leveraging maps from other (current or complete) programs with similar stakeholders as a starting point. If other similar work has been performed in the same organization, interview the Program Manager, team members and review "lessons learned" documents. Even if the work is not the same, you may glean some insight relative to preferences of stakeholders you haven't yet interacted.

## Use the Appropriate Communications Type

As stated above, one of the scarcest resources in business is management time. The whole team should plan the appropriate medium to communicate based on the needs of the stakeholders (e.g., Program Intranet site, Program Dashboards, Self-Service standard presentations, External Internet site, Office Hours, Meetings, etc.). Consider:

- If an Instant message will suffice, do not hold a meeting.
- If a meeting is needed, validate the participants have a compelling need to attend.
- Hold the meeting for the appropriate amount of time. If 15 minutes is all that is needed, then schedule as such.
- Maintain informal communications to engage as appropriate. Please note it is especially important to build trusted business relationships with key stakeholders. People will always provide a bit more levity with those they like when things get tough; and less with those they haven't yet developed a trust.

## Provide "Self-Service" Communications

Not every interaction needs to be face-to-face. A program intranet site should be available and structured in a way that the stakeholders can most readily access information that is pertinent to their needs. The site should accommodate three levels of information: Executive,

Program and Delivery team with role-based access control to ensure information protection as appropriate.

Often programs like to have their own "brand identity" or codename for esprit de corps. While the codename helps generate feelings of pride, fellowship, and common loyalty shared by the members of the program, it is important not to lose the bigger brand – that of the organization (e.g., Company Name, Agency, etc.). The program should always apply the organization's visual identity standards in all communications. The visual identity system creates a "look" that applies the consistent use of logos, colors and typography. By using internal templates and standards, the program can focus on the content and not the container.

### *Apply Meeting Best Practices*

Have you ever been in a meeting that you left and said, "What was that about?" or "Why did I go to that meeting?" or even "What a waste of time that was!" While the list below may be intuitive, it is helpful to reinforce these best practices to ensure that everyone's time is optimized. Hopefully by applying the techniques below others will follow and there will be fewer questions relative to the value of some meetings.

- **Validate key attendees are available**: Prior to scheduling or conducting a meeting. If a key resource or decision-maker is not available, it is often better to reschedule a meeting for a time that they are available. So much time is lost due to ineffective meetings. This time could be applied to other productive activities.

- **Always have an agenda for meetings**: Having an agenda will drive who should attend (and possibly who should not) and will help keep the meetings on subject.

- **Schedule only the time needed**: Most meetings are scheduled for 30 or 60 minutes in part due to culture and in part due to the ease of creating meetings using the calendar software defaults (30, 60 minutes). If only 15 minutes is required, consider setting up a 15-minute meeting v. 30-minute meeting. Also consider if a separate meeting is even required, see below on AOB.

- **Use AOB on agendas:** To reduce the total number of meetings, consider adding *Any Other Business*

(AOB) to meeting agendas. Not every topic warrants a separate meeting. As teams hold meetings, consider if time permits, a discussion on related or quick hit topics. Using AOB is another way to increase productivity.

# Chapter 14:
# Quality Management

Program Quality Management ensures the organization is best positioned to satisfy the needs of stakeholders and deliver the intended outcomes and benefits for which it was chartered while ensuring the performing organization

> **Quality Management**
> Has three primary goals:
> 1) Satisfy the needs of stakeholders.
> 2) Deliver the intended outcomes and benefits for which it was chartered.
> 3) While ensuring the performing organization does not incur unnecessary significant risks.

does not incur significant risks. Quality management mechanisms are emplaced throughout the program life cycle; and the program outcomes are transitioned to an operational state in a manner to ensure the required quality standards are maintained afterward. The lack of an effective quality management system often results in detrimental effects throughout the life cycle (rework, cost overruns, etc.) and ultimately upon delivery (low stakeholder satisfaction, lack of acceptance and use of the outcomes, etc.). Program Quality Management supports the work of the delivery teams by providing governance and maintaining common standards and processes.

There are a multitude of definitions for quality. Three noted authors and quality experts, Joseph M Juran, Philip B Crosby, and W. Edward Deming, are often quoted for their contributions and definitions of quality. Juran, the "Father of Quality," defined quality as "fitness for use." He stated, "the product should be a good price, work well for the customer, be distributed efficiently from the producer to the customer, and be supported efficiently by the company" (O'Grady, 2021). Crosby, best known for the "Zero Defects" concept, wrote quality means "conformance to requirements" (Crosby 1979). He further states there are no "levels" of quality, whereas it is a binary condition that the requirement was met or not. Deming, an American engineer, is best known for his management consulting work with Japanese businesses where he developed and introduced the PDCA (Plan, Do, Check, Act) method. Deming's stance on quality is that ""Quality is defined from the customer's point of view as anything that enhances their satisfaction" (Deming, 1986). The collective works of Juran, Crosby, and Deming are still applied in quality management methods today.

## Scope of Quality in Programs

The International Organization for Standardization (ISO) provides standards that "offer solutions and best practices for almost all types of technology and business, helping companies and organizations to increase performance while protecting consumers and the planet" (Dodd, 2021). In 1987, ISO introduced an international standard that provides requirements for a Quality Management System they termed ISO:9001. The standard has been updated over the years via a consensus process and today's version was last updated in 2015 (ISO 9001:2015). Today, ISO 9001:2015 is the quality standard used by "over one million companies and organizations in over 170 countries" (ISO, 2022). The ISO 9001 quality standard is used by: Construction, Engineering, Technology services, Manufacturing, Hotels & Hospitality, Community services, Health, and many other industries (St. Clair, 2022).

Each of ISO's (ISO 9001:2015) seven quality management principles presented in Figure 21 are intended to improve an organization's performance in the area noted. The core focus on customers harkens back to some to the writings of authors referenced earlier, in that the customer is core to defining and accepting outcomes to their level, perception, and expectations of quality. Each principle is mapped to the directly to specific benefits and the program management practices that support these principles. The seven principles are related to the areas of quality management for organizations in general and can be used to define the scope of quality for programs.

The ISO model provides insights into the scope of the work performed in programs relative to quality. By considering the work of the authors and ISO, this information has been consolidated into three core impact areas for programs as:

- **Stakeholder Quality:** Customer Focus, Leadership, Engagement of People and Relationship Management (Suppliers and Business Partners);
- **Product and Service Quality:** Quality of the change activity outcome – fitness for use; and

- **Process Quality:** Process approach, improvements, and evidenced-based decisions.

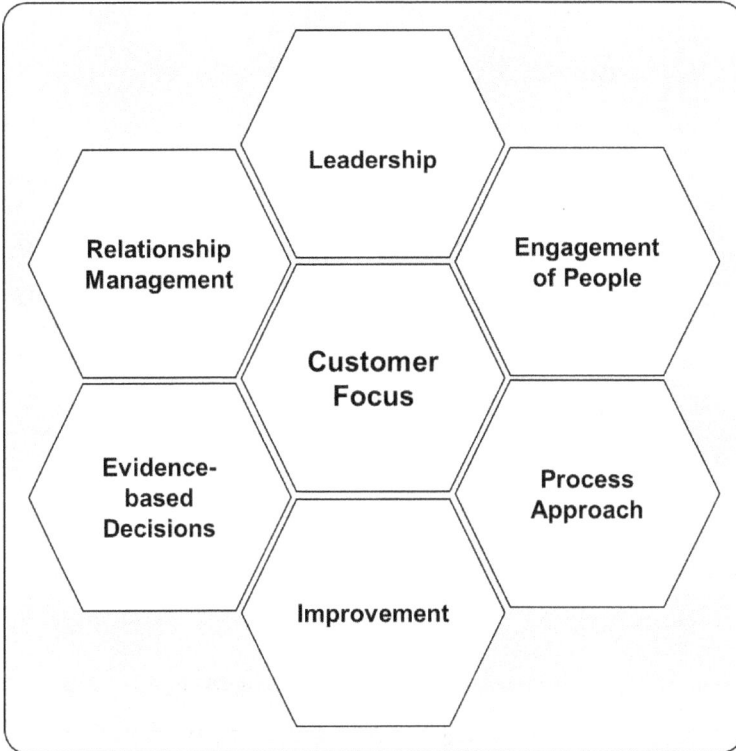

*Figure 21.* ISO's Seven Quality Management Principles can be used as a foundation to guide an organization's performance improvement (ISO, 2015). Reprinted with permission.

### *Stakeholder Quality*

The primary focus of program quality management is to meet customer requirements, both stated and implied, and deliver outcomes that provide "fitness for use" and are adopted by the customer while striving to exceed their expectations. Program (and organizational) success is achieved through a laser focus on the customer. Customer confidence and trust are measured through customer satisfaction metrics (net promoter scores, interview results), repeat business, expanded customer based (word of mouth advertising), increased revenue and market share. Through these relationships, over time, additional value can be created for the customer, and subsequently for the performing organization. As the customer base grows, more information is gathered, leading to a stronger understanding of the customer's current and future needs.

Leadership at all levels needs to ensure people are informed, aligned, engaged, and empowered to provide the best value for their individual needs and goals, those of the customer, and those of the organization. By providing the appropriate opportunities (and training), effectiveness and efficiency gains are realized resulting in increased quality outcomes.

Suppliers and business partners play a crucial role in an organization's success. For instance, Ford introduced the One Ford initiative in 2007 to standardize their products on a global level and strengthen their relationship with suppliers. According to Putre (2016), Ford states that they regularly communicate to their suppliers the types of technologies and product innovations that interest them, which helps suppliers prioritize their investments, R&D spending, and resource allocation. This provides the suppliers greater opportunities to focus on their customer's current and future needs while Ford can rapidly innovate their product lines by leveraging this community to differentiate their global products based on the ideas that come forward.

### *Product and Service Quality*

Product and Service Quality focuses on providing program outcomes that meet the "fit for use" and conformance to requirements specifications. The change activities (aka program outcomes) are generally provided by delivery teams. However, the program team may directly develop processes and lead change activities that are under the guidance of a quality management system. The program team's primary role (as related to delivery teams) is to govern the overall process across teams and ensure the appropriate process (e.g., The Deming Cycle [PDCA]) is followed appropriately and results are acted upon. Depending upon the product or service the specific attributes or measures of quality may differ. This is discussed later in the process section below.

### *Process Quality*

Process quality refers to the process used to govern or create the change activities products. It can also refer to the change activity itself if the goal is to change or improve a process (vs. create a product, service, etc.). Consistent and predictable results are achieved more effectively and efficiently when activities are standardized, and the teams receive the appropriate support (e.g., Training, Process Documentation, etc.).

Continuous improvement is essential for an organization to respond to internal findings and external opportunities to increase efficiency and overall effectiveness. Improvements are most effective when the focus on prevention vs. correction. An improvement in preventative actions may reduce or obviate the need for changes to a corrective process. This is in line with

Crosby's Do it Right the First Time (DRIFT) approach and Juran's application of the Pareto Principle to quality (where 80% of the issues arise from 20% of the problems).

Evidenced-based (or data-driven) decisions can reduce some uncertainty inherent in the decision-making process. When assessing opportunities for process improvements, it is important to understand the complexity of interrelated processes to avoid unintended consequences. For example, imagine taking the restraint system out of a roller coaster because some customers find it uncomfortable. By sacrificing conformance to regulatory, security, safety, or other customer requirements to improve a user experience is a myopic view and one that can only lead to dissatisfaction (or much worse) in the end. Brainstorming exercises, rapid prototypes, modeling, and simulation data can provide innovations that still conform to the requirements while enhancing the user experience by building more comfortable restraints.

## Quality Management Process

The quality management process comprises an overall governance function and core processes to validate and verify quality outcomes from the program and delivery teams. From a governance perspective, the program team reviews and approves of the quality approach and supports the delivery teams by providing or verifying the following resources are in place:

- Program level quality requirements including standardized processes for quality management activities;
- Organizational or industry specific requirements beyond stated individual customer requirements (e.g., Regulatory, Security, etc.);
- Access to the appropriate resources (e.g., financial, facilities, human, material, technology, etc.) to conduct quality processes; and
- Standard measures to validate the quality requirements.

The scope of quality processes includes stakeholders, products and services, and processes within a program regardless of the performing team. This means processes developed and maintained by the program team as well as the change activities performed by the delivery teams need to follow a quality management process. As introduced earlier in this chapter, the Deming Cycle (See Figure 22) is a very commonly applied quality management approach, and it is the core approach for ISO 9001:2015.

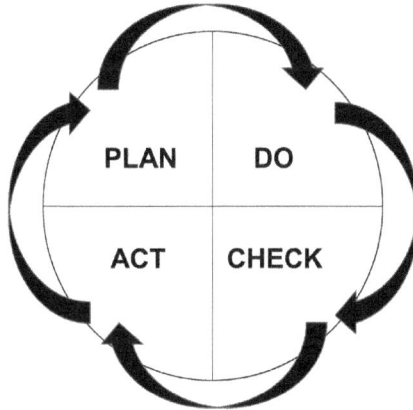

*Figure 22.* The Deming Cycle (PDCA) is a commonly used approach to quality management and process improvement. Reprinted with permission.

As depicted above, the Deming Cycle (PDCA) is an ongoing process where the team will iterate the cycle for each assessment performed. The Deming Cycle aligns with Juran's Trilogy in that quality planning in represented in Deming's "Plan," quality control in Deming's "Check," and quality improvement in Deming's "Act." The specific work performed is dependent upon many variables that include the team capabilities, level of risk, the change(s) itself, available facilities tools and equipment, and many other potential constraints. The activities of each phase can be briefly described as:

- **Plan:** This is where the requirements of the change activity are elicited and defined. This information drives the type of resources needed to deliver the outcome, measures to ensure the change activity conforms to customer's and organization's requirements, and the identification of initial risks.
- **Do:** The change activity is created. Measurements are refined at this time. This may also be a time for the quality team to receive training on new methods, processes, or standards to apply to the outcomes under consideration.
- **Check:** In this phase the outcome of the change activity is measured to determine if the actual results conform to the expected results.
- **Act:** In this phase, the "evidence-based" results are assessed, and actions are documented.

Plans are then developed, and actions taken to make preventative (preferred) or corrective changes to minimize the undesired outcomes in future iterations. Depending upon the change activity, the PDCA process may iterate many times following preventative or corrective actions that have been applied until the desired outcomes are achieved.

There are many quality management approaches that can be applied and followed based on the requirements of the performing organization or the change activities themselves. The PDCA method above was selected because it applies to a broad base of change activities and with ISO's adoption and over 1 million companies using this approach, it seemed appropriate for this book. Others for consideration may include:

- **Capability Maturity Model Integration (CMMI)** "helps organizations quickly understand their current level of capability and performance in the context of their own business objectives and compared to similar organizations" (ISACA, 2022).
- **Failure Modes and Effects Analysis (FMEA)** can be used either proactively when developing a design, function or process or responding to an

incident. The term failure "modes" infers the "mode or way" something may fail; where effects analysis is reviewing and identifying the root cause of that failure (American Society for Quality, 2022).

- The **House of Quality** (part of the Quality Function Deployment) where customers "desires" are documented and correlated with engineering capabilities "hows" derive functional and non-functional (service, etc.) requirements.

- **Kaizen** is a continuous process improvement method that "focuses on eliminating waste, improving productivity, and achieving sustained continual improvement in targeted activities and processes of an organization" (US EPA, 2021).

- The **Six Sigma DMAIC** method is a five-step approach primarily used for process improvement. Using this approach you Define the problem, Measure its impacts, Analyze the root causes, Improve the process, and finally Control by monitoring the environment. The cycle can iterate until a desired state is achieved.

While this was not an exhaustive list, the items above represent the most common methods I've seen over my years in information technology. Manufacturing, construction, energy, and other industries may apply many other methods.

## Techniques for Agility in Quality Management

Today's Agile methods provide many opportunities to positively impact quality outcomes for the change activities being produced. Through rapid prototypes and Minimum Viable Products (MVPs) (for products/software) or structured walkthroughs (for processes), the customer can quickly respond to the delivery team's interpretation of their requirements. This provides an opportunity for early changes and helps satisfy the quality standards of both "fit for use" and "customer's perception of quality." The primary organizational agility theme associated with quality management is *organizational competency*. Considerations to improve agility in quality management at the program level include:

### *Establish a Quality Culture*

David Ratnaraj said in his 2014 PMI conference paper that "Quality in software development is often an afterthought. Most software projects assume quality is engrained in the development process, only to encounter major quality issues during the test and deployment phases." I have seen first-hand on many occasions where defects found in testing are not fully resolved due to insufficient time to recode and retest before deadlines. This often results in software delivered with IOUs on defect resolution.

A Culture of Quality is both a top-down and bottom-up venture. Keeping an eye on the big picture can help facilitate collaboration among teams. Using today's agile methods, multiple teams may be working concurrently on different portions of the same system. The cumulative effect of change on change or over time significant changes may necessitate a change to the underlying architecture. The system may begin to slow, thus affecting the perceived quality for the customer. By keeping an eye on the big picture, understanding upcoming changes, and facilitating collaboration among teams, the cumulative changes to the overall system can also be accommodated while continuing to provide new and enhanced customer requirements without impacting the overall system.

### *Provide Quality Management Training*

To have teams better understand their role in the Quality Culture, they need to be provided with the appropriate training in program processes and standards. The standards may include organizational, industry specific and/or legal and regulatory standards and requirements. For example, when the Health Insurance Portability and Accountability Act of 1996 (HIPAA), was passed, it represented a significant change in which individually identifiable health information was required to be protected by those in the industry. Considerations for confidentiality, integrity, and availability of electronic protected health information not only impacted the institutions who stored this electronic information but also impacted how it could be shared (U.S. Department of Health & Human Services, 2022). The program team needs to remain aware of similar changes in their industry in addition to internal standards to minimize organizational risks.

In many cases, the standards are not new, but may be new to the program team members. In this case, the program may leverage standards or training from other prior or existing programs to accelerate the process of documenting organizational requirements. By reusing processes rather than creating new, not only will you complete faster, but the new materials may also be more aligned to the processes (and policies) of that specific organization.

### *Build a Competency in Quality*

Depending upon the length of time the program is expected to support multiple delivery efforts, this may yield new opportunities to centralize quality management functions to achieve economies of scale and reduce overall costs. Rather than having each delivery team have their own dedicated quality management team.

By building a committed Quality Management team within the program that serves multiple teams, several benefits become available. Many studies show that new teams mature over time. Consider Bruce W. Tuckman's theory that teams go through a series of phases that include forming, storming, norming, and performing (Tuckman, 1965). When a program first starts up, the same processes are generally followed. Based on this model, a team's efficiency and productivity is highest when they execute at the performing stage. To get the team to the performing stage quickly, all team members should have a common understanding of the organizational and program goals and objectives (Ratnaraj, 2014). Then by creating a centralized competency, as new delivery teams exit and new ones arise, the institutional knowledge will remain within the quality management team.

The Quality team, working in conjunction with the Information Management team, should define and implement metrics and dashboards that provide visibility into progress and performance. This can help teams become "self-policing" where they can identify areas for improvement and course correct as needed.

Program Management Redefined

# Chapter 15:

# Organizational Change Management

Each change activity undertaken is only as successful as its integration and acceptance following the delivery lifecycle. Without effective organizational change management (OCM), company transitions can be rocky and expensive in terms of both time and resources. Ultimately, "a lack of effective change management can lead the organization to failure" (Stobierski, 2020).

> ***Organizational Change*** may come in many forms:
> - Strategic
> - Structural
> - People-centered
> - Transformational
> - Unplanned
> - Remedial
>
> Applying the appropriate methods and properly engaging those affected can help reduce resistance and lead to active support.

Depending upon the specifics of the change activity, several organizations or (internal or external) stakeholders may be involved or impacted. For example, if an organization moves their primary data center operations to the cloud. While the cloud services may be familiar to the team of people who supported the services in the on-premises data center, their roles may change considering the (new cloud based) systems may now be supported by an external cloud services organization or some other hybrid arrangement. For some in the former data center support role, their job may change to an oversight function the oversee the new cloud provider is meeting the conditions of their contract. Others may be retrained for other functions in the organization. While others may be incented to help with the migration effort and receive a severance package or early retirement package once the work is complete. Some will leave immediately; others won't stay long. It is very important to get this right. Not all changes have this level of impact, many (likely most) are simply enhancements to existing efforts, while others involve outsourcing efforts (as described above) or automating processes where there are significant impacts to the people, processes, and products of an organization.

In any of the cases presented above, if the change involves a significant change to an employee role or position, Human Resources, Labor Unions, legal teams, and others may be involved. For most change activities, there is a minimum requirement to provide communications, trainings, and/or support requirements as the stewardship of the change is transitioned from the delivery to operations teams. With changes impacting external stakeholders, for example a major vendor provides a new version of their software product, there is a whole community that is involved from testing activities prior to its release and additional communications, marketing, support, and other requirements during the initial phases of the launch.

It is important to note that despite an organization's best efforts to manage change, there will be times that the change isn't fully (or at all) adopted by the intended end users. In fact, there is a frequently quoted statistic from McKinsey Publishing "that about 70 percent of organizational-change programs fail to meet their objectives." That leaves 30 percent that succeed based on a study of over 2500 organizations (London, 2019). The statistics are relative to significant organizational change and consistent with the writings of E.M. Rogers' 1962 Diffusion of Innovation theory.

Rogers noted that the adoption of a new idea, behavior, or product (i.e., "innovation") does not happen simultaneously in a social system; rather it is a process whereby some people are more apt to adopt the innovation than others (Lamorte, 2022). The five categories show that people assimilate changes at different rates. The first 16%, Innovators (2.5%) and Early Adopters (13.5%) of the population will likely embrace and adopt change much faster than the remaining 84% of the population.

But this is related to significant changes, this can't be the same for incremental changes, right? Brent Gleeson (2017) wrote in Forbes that the number one reason for failure in his study was "Change Battle Fatigue." He cited similar statistics (to the slow adoption of innovations), and he described the following contributing factors to the high failure rates:

- A weak culture that isn't aligned with the mission;
- Lack of participation and buy-in;
- Under-communicating a powerful vision;
- Over-communicating a poor vision;

- Not enough training or resources; and
- Change Battle Fatigue.

Change battle fatigue is the result of many elements such as past failures plaguing the minds of employees and the sacrifices made during the arduous change process. When a transformation is poorly led, fatigue can set in quickly. Research has shown that there are several reasons for the extremely high failure rate but also some strategies to increase that success rate. Strategies for success include may include (Emerson, 2022):

- Invest significant time and energy into creating a comprehensive change management strategy before starting any change initiative. Several models are presented in this Chapter.
- Revisit your strategy plan frequently and continuously assess and change as appropriate.
- Keep messages simple, on point, and ongoing. Opportunities for success fizzle out when leaders do not communicate enough after the initiative is announced.

- Identify potential sources of resistance from the start. Plan strategies to address them. Actively listen to and engage your stakeholders throughout the change.
- Ensure your change strategy is grounded in a realistic assessment of your organization's culture and vision.
- Managing expectations—both positive and negative.
- Celebrate short- and mid-term wins!

## Scope of OCM in Programs

There are varying accounts on the number of types of change in organizations. Some authors discuss five, while others present up to 12 types of organizational change. After reviewing and consolidating, six types of organizational changes are presented below (SweetProcess, 2019; Stobierski, 2021; Shaban, 2022):

- **Strategic Change:** A major change in the strategy of an organization to reflect change in customer wants and needs. Example: A car company that changes to alternative fuel powered cars only.
- **Organizational Structural Change:** A significant change to how the organization is structured and

the resources are aligned with that new structure. This may be a result of a merger or significant changes in the market requiring a new business area. An organizational structure may also change to align with a new way of working (e.g., Agile@Scale).

- **People-center Changes:** When an organization undergoes significant increased hiring or staff reductions. In response to market conditions.

- **Transformational Change:** Involves a significant change in what products and services an organization provides. DISH Networks is entering the consumer cellular and wireless networking markets. This could be considered both a strategy and transformational, however, it was placed here as their strategy has been communications centered, and this is transformational in that it is a new product line under their expanded strategy.

- **Unplanned Change:** This may be as a part of a change in laws related to that organization, an unfavorable ruling in an antitrust case, product recalls, or a key resource leaving the organization.

- **Remedial Change:** Most changes in organizations are of this type. These are generally incremental changes to products, services, processes, etc., that support customers changing needs.

While all types of organizational change have an impact on programs, the risk tolerance and maturity of the specific industry will dictate the type of changes the program team will most likely undertake. Some will find themselves involved in significant transformational changes while others may focus on maturing their current offerings and find themselves focused on remedial changes. Regardless of the type of change it is important for the program team to "stay in their lane" relative to their involvement at the portfolio and delivery team levels.

Organizational Change Management at the program level is not intended to replace OCM efforts at the delivery team level, but to augment, coordinate, or supplement them as appropriate. Many program management books, standards, and references do not specifically address this area as a requirement, placing the burden on the individual delivery teams and subsequent impacts on the stakeholders.

Deploying multiple changes separately, and potentially at different times, could create a greater burden for the business than through fewer coordinated and planned deliveries. Considering programs have insight into and governance over several change activities, there is an opportunity to plan the deployment of multiple changes concurrently and prepare for and mitigate these impacts on the stakeholders and business communities affected by the changes.

## OCM Processes

There are many models used specifically in the organizational change management process. From those that support full organizational structural change (e.g., McKinsey 7-S Model [Strategy, Structure, Systems, Style, Staff, Skills, Surrounding Shared Values]) (Peters & Waterman, 1982) to those for personal or small group change (e.g., Elisabeth Kübler-Ross (1969) Change Curve [including: denial, frustration, depression, experiment, decision, and integration]) adapted from her original *"5 stages of grief."* Additional models including ADKAR (Awareness, Desire, Knowledge, Ability and Reinforcement), Bridges Transition Model (Endings, Neutral Zone, New Beginnings), Maurer's Change Model

(Three Levels of Resistance), Nudge Theory (i.e., using indirect techniques to influence behavior), and Satir were considered, however, I've primarily seen four models used on programs and have selected Deming's PDCA, Lewin's Change Management Model, Kotter's 8-step Change Model and the emerging Lean Change Management model as representative OCM models for consideration. The Deming PDCA Model, which was previously discussed in the Quality Management Chapter (14), can be easily adapted by using the steps for organizational change-oriented activities. A brief overview of the other selected models follows.

### Lewin's Change Management Model

Kurt Lewin, considered the founder of modern social psychology (Cherry, 2020), developed one of the earliest models for organizational change that is still in use today, Lewin's Change Management Model (1947). As depicted in Figure 23, Lewin's three phase model included processes for 1) Unfreezing 2) Changing and 3) Refreezing the environmental variables for change resulting in the acceptance and sustainment of organizational changes. I can imagine that you may be thinking, *"really, Program Management Redefined and you're presenting a method from 1947."* Please stay with this chapter to the end and you'll see the relevance. Even Lewin (1951) himself stated "There is nothing so practical as a good theory." Some best practices indeed stand the test of time.

In the "unfreezing" phase, the organizational change management team supports the overall strategic direction by first helping to create the perception that a change is needed. The core concept is that if people feel involved and better understand that the status quo is hindering the organization (or their specific work), they may be more interested in seeing and potentially participating in the change. More awareness and interest in the change will help those involved or impacted become more motivated and better see the urgency to support the change.

In the "change" phase, plans are developed, and activities commence in support of that new desired organizational construct, process, level of behavior or change outcome. Communications are disseminated, training and development initiatives are provided, and the team moves toward the desired change. Finally, in the "refreezing" phase the new behaviors are solidified, processes are normalized, and the organizational structures and other changes are now accepted as the new status quo.

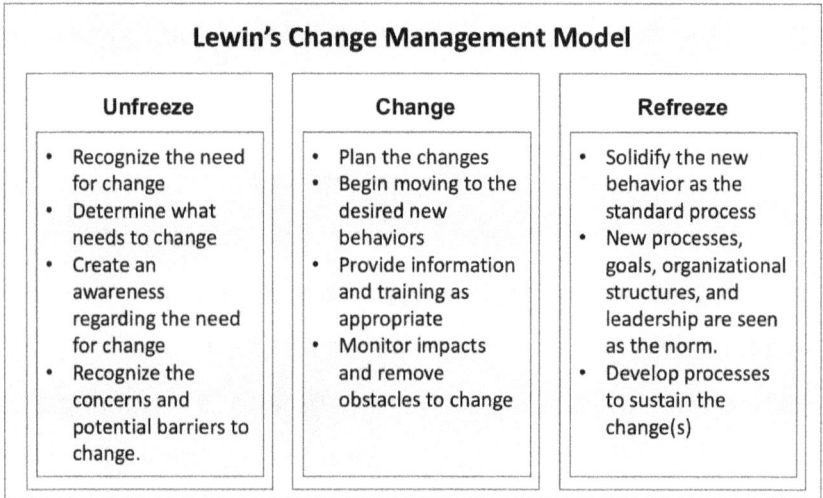

| Lewin's Change Management Model | | |
| --- | --- | --- |
| **Unfreeze** | **Change** | **Refreeze** |
| • Recognize the need for change<br>• Determine what needs to change<br>• Create an awareness regarding the need for change<br>• Recognize the concerns and potential barriers to change. | • Plan the changes<br>• Begin moving to the desired new behaviors<br>• Provide information and training as appropriate<br>• Monitor impacts and remove obstacles to change | • Solidify the new behavior as the standard process<br>• New processes, goals, organizational structures, and leadership are seen as the norm.<br>• Develop processes to sustain the change(s) |

*Figure 23*. Lewin's Change Management Model (1947) is a commonly used approach to guide organizational change management initiatives. Reprinted with permission.

While some describe organizational change as an ongoing process where refreezing isn't truly possible, others describe this as the sustainment portion of the refreezing process. I submit that without some semblance of a baseline, there is only chaos, and not a changeable improvable environment.

### Kotter's 8-Step Change Model

John Paul Kotter, a Harvard Business School Professor Emeritus and a world-renowned change expert introduced an 8-step change process in his 1996 book *Leading Change*. The model was developed based on his research of over 100 organizations which were going through significant change. The 8-steps include (Kotter, 2022):

1. **Create a Sense of Urgency:** Inspire people to act – with passion and purpose – to achieve a bold, aspirational opportunity. Build momentum that excites people to pursue a compelling (and clear) vision of the future… together.

2. **Build a Guiding Coalition:** A volunteer network needs a coalition of committed people – born of its own ranks – to guide it, coordinate it, and communicate its activities.

3. **Form a Strategic Vision:** Clarify how the future will be different from the past and get buy-in for how you can make that future a reality through initiatives linked directly to the vision.

4. **Enlist a Volunteer Army:** Large-scale change can only occur when massive numbers of people rally

around a common opportunity. At an individual level, they must want to actively contribute. Collectively, they must be unified in the pursuit of achieving the goal together.

5. **Enable Action by Removing Barriers:** Remove the obstacles that slow things down or create roadblocks to progress. Clear the way for people to innovate, work more nimbly across silos, and generate impact quickly.

6. **Generate Short-Term Wins:** Wins are the molecules of results. They must be recognized, collected, and communicated – early and often – to track progress and energize volunteers to persist.

7. **Sustain Acceleration:** The way that you can assure success using this method is not to skip any of the steps or the learnings.

8. **Institute Change:** Articulate the connections between new behaviors and organizational success, making sure they continue until they become strong enough to replace old habits. Evaluate systems and processes to ensure management practices reinforce the new behaviors, mindsets, and ways of working you invested in.

There are several similarities between Lewin's and Kotter's models. As depicted in Figure 24, the outside circles show Kotter's 8-steps, and the inside sections align those steps with Lewin's model.

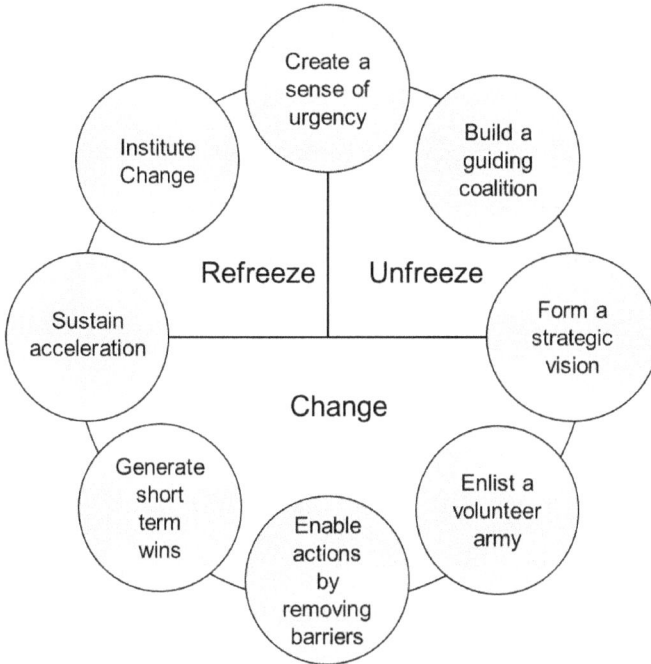

*Figure 24.* An overlay of Lewin's and Kotter's models shows a consistency between Lewin's 1947 model and the 2022 version of Kotter's 8-step model.

Kotter's model has specific advantages and disadvantages. The advantages include that it is indeed a step-by-step model, making it easy to follow and implement. By including employees at the heart of the change, resistance is generally lower and acceptance higher. The advantages may also serve as disadvantages. Since it is a step-by-step process, each step is dependent upon the prior step. Steps cannot be skipped. Some also say it is time-consuming. Finally, it is top-down oriented, which limits the viewpoints and opportunities for co-creation.

### Lean Change Management Model

Resistance to change is a natural reaction when you don't involve people affected by the change. Jason Little's book, *Lean Change Management*, shows how to implement successful change through examples of innovative practices that can dramatically improve the success of change programs (Goncalves, 2022). Little's methods focus on successfully implementing change and bypassing change resistance by co-creating change.

The Lean Change Management Model is multi-layered and has a core set of 5 "Universals" which read as guiding principles. These include (LCM, 2022):

- **Cause & Purpose:** We value Cause and Purpose over Urgency for Change.
- **Experimentation:** We believe in experimenting our way through change over executing tasks in a plan.
- **Co-Creation:** We believe in co-creating change over getting buy-in through coercion.
- **Meaningful Dialogue:** We believe in enabling meaningful dialogue over broadcasting information at people.
- **Response to Change:** We believe in understanding the response to change over blaming people for resisting.

The method does leverage other previously developed and industry recognized methods, however, I found this method interesting in the way it centers on co-creation. Across a career of consulting, I've always recognized that the internal teams best understand the issues and best way forward (than the 50-mile experts).

## Techniques for Agility in OCM

By reviewing the type of change the organization is undertaking and understanding the specifics of each of the models provided above, the organizational change manager can customize a plan based on their specific organizational change requirements. Additional techniques for organizational agility in this area should be considered when developing the plan. This practice area most closely aligns with the organizational agility theme of *strategic alignment and responsiveness.*

### *Foster a Culture of Change*

While the OCM methods described above focus on specific changes, it is so important to foster a (respectful) culture of change where it is seen as constant, necessary, and positive. The term "Change Agility" refers to systems and a culture of change that supports the ability (and agility) to accommodate change. This includes cultural elements including feedback mechanisms where employees can engage either one-on-one, in groups or communities of interest, or via forums where anonymous feedback can be provided without fear of reprisal.

Many organizations invest in systems and strategies and do not realize the full benefits they set out to achieve because they did not consider the OCM aspects of change. Integrating change management activities early in your planning will significantly improve the success of your implementation. From a program perspective, the impending changes across the delivery teams should be aggregated, depicted on a roadmap, and planned to understand the cumulative impacts to various stakeholder communities. This cross team, big picture view can reveal many issues and opportunities for planning. Regardless of the method chosen, consider the tenants of Little's "5 Universals" (i.e., Cause & Purpose, Experimentation, Co-Creation, Meaningful Dialogue, and Response to Change). These undoubtedly will reduce resistance and improve acceptance.

# Chapter 16:
# Resource Management

A critical activity for Program Managers is to apply resources (e.g., financial, facilities, human, material, technology, etc.) to the highest priority change activities based on the strategic value they provide to the sponsoring organization. When resource management is properly performed, your organization can realize reduced costs, improved efficiencies, and productivity increases.

> ***Resource Budgeting***
> "Spend the money as if it's your own" is the advice I give all involved in budgeting. If you can identify and use available or shared resources, consider this before expending funds on any new resources. Remember, the budget you receive is an investment in the program and the efficiency and effectiveness of the usage is a major factor in measuring the program's (and your) success.

The goal of Program Resource Management is to use the right mix of resources to satisfy requirements while understanding that these same resources are likely in demand elsewhere in the business. There are often situations when a Program Manager faces difficult decisions relative to the use of resources to the detriment of another change activity. Before deciding, the program manager (or decision maker) should elicit information from the appropriate stakeholders to gather relevant information. Once information is collected, they often meet with or consult the sponsor and/or other key stakeholders to arrive at an informed decision. If the decision is made to support one at the risk of another change activity and overall, and this will help the organization achieve its highest priority goals more effectively the tradeoff is justifiable (Harrin, 2022). Certainly, other alternatives (e.g., reallocating or securing additional resources) must be exhausted before considering such a tradeoff.

While human and financial resources are often the most discussed resource types, information/information management and material resource allocation must also be considered.

# Scope of Program Resource Management

The program budget supports the resources to support the program itself and all allocated delivery teams and change activities. Having a full understanding (and accounting) of the required scope at the onset of a program lays the foundation to ensuring resources are appropriately allocated and optimized to support the highest priority change initiatives based on their alignment to the strategic plan. This is an ongoing activity as change activities are completed and new activities are initiated. The scope of Program Resource Management considers the sum of the resources required for the change activities in the program along with those to support the program management activities themselves (directly or indirectly). Resource categories include people, material, information/information management, and financial resources.

## *Financial Resources*

Includes the sum of all funding needed to support the resources listed above. It is also important to consider the costs involved in the acquisition and onboarding of resources over time. Sometimes they are covered by the program, other times they are part of an organization's general and administrative overhead costs. This factor could be significant and should be known how they are covered to make sure this doesn't become an issue.

### Facilities Resources

Facilities include provisions for physical or virtual space for people, products, or equipment. The supporting equipment is often included in the inventory of facilities budgets. This equipment may include office automation and communications equipment (e.g., conference call products, virtual white boards, etc.). If all employees work remotely, there may be a requirement to provide (budget for) products or services to facilitate this arrangement.

### People (aka Human) Resources

Includes internal and external human resources who provide direct or indirect support. Internal resources may come from existing resources or new hires. External resources may be obtained via contract, sub-contract, or consulting sources. Indirect human resource costs may include funding those in an audit, oversight, governance, or management support capacity. Other types of resources may require program funding based on the requirements and processes of performing organization.

## *Material Resources*

Material resources include physical or virtual materials, machines, tools, equipment, software, facilities, etc. These materials may include consumables such as office supplies, 3D printing materials, etc. Virtual describes computing resources to include virtual cloud material (e.g., virtual machines [VMs]), software, networking, security, and other virtual services. When considering the cost of cloud or on premises computing, be sure to include all required environments (e.g., sandbox, POC, Dev, Test, Int, etc.).

## *Technology Resources*

Technology resources include hardware, software, subscriptions, or online resources that produce, manipulate, process, store, communicate, or disseminate information. They are often spoken of in terms of hardware, software, firmware, and services regardless of their source (e.g., physical, virtual, or cloud based). Personal computers are often included in this budget. The services many also include information management solutions.

Information/information management resources may include subscription services for information resources (e.g., credit ratings, company information listings, research, etc.) or tools for Information Management. Information management resources include products to support the management of the program itself or the products built within the program (e.g., Application Lifecycle Management [ALM]/Enterprise Agile Planning [EAP]) licenses and subscriptions, Data and Document repositories, Internet/Intranet tools, Process Assess Libraries, etc. Because of the vast array of considerations for information resources, it is listed as a separate program practice in Chapter 17: Information Management.

## Program Resource Management Process

Program Resource Management includes practices to plan, acquire, allocate, manage, optimize, and release resources. The subsections that follow provide additional information regarding the work performed in each process area.

## *Resource Planning*

Resource planning includes activities to identify and quantify the resources required to support both the program team and those resources needed at the delivery level. The first step is to understand the resources required for a program. The list below provides some potential factors Program Managers should consider when defining the initial scope of resources required (Stobierski, 2021):

- The type of resources needed (e.g., financial, facilities, human, material, technology, etc.);
- The amount of each resource needed;
- The source of resources (internal/external);
- The timing of when resources are required;
- The lead time required for the resource (e.g., for Human resources, Onboarding time including interviewing, on-boarding, etc.; for material resources, product availability, production timing, supply chain lead time, etc.);
- The cost associated with the resources;
- The method to ensure the resources are managed efficiently;
- The metrics used to monitor and assess each resource; and

- The process used to release resources.

Following the identification, the type and quantity of resources required, an initial budget is drafted. Considering the work is often unique with some inherent or anticipated risk and uncertainty, the budget should include a factor for management reserve (also known as "contingency"). This contingency funding should represent a relatively small amount of the total budget to accommodate the "unknown unknowns." The actual percentage or amount is dependent on the risk and uncertainty factors discussed in the risk/issue management chapter.

The risk managed budget, along with supporting information, is presented the sponsoring organization often in a business case format as discussed in the Strategic Alignment chapter of this book. As discussed, the initial Program Business Case provides the justification for the investment in the program. It often includes the: Requested Budget, Justification, Objectives, Strategic contribution, Achievability assessment, Key deliverables, Risks, Resource requirements, Impact on organization, and Cost Benefits Analysis.

Developing and submitting a budget does not ensure the budget will be approved. This is often an iterative process, where the Program Manager assesses and presents alternatives to minimize the requested budget. In some organizations, the cost of capital (cost to borrow) is also a factor. If the return on investment does not cover the cost of the investment plus interest, the work may not be funded. If the business case meets the business needs and provides the proper return on investment, it is likely it will be approved. Once the budget is approved, the acquisition and allocation activities may begin.

### *Resource Acquisition and Allocation*

Resources may be obtained through several sources. Prior to seeking new resources for work, be sure to exhaust opportunities to leverage shared or existing resources that have capacity. For people, this may be checking if someone (or a group) has unused capacity for the work being proposed. For material resources, consider leveraging the assets already in place (e.g., available cloud storage, shared resources, extra space in an office [or remote work], etc.).

The program team should work with the appropriate organizations to secure the resources required. These may include Human Capital (Resource) Management, Legal (for Non-Disclosure Agreements and New Contracts or extensions), Contracts (for existing suppliers of people, materials, or information-related resources), Procurement (aka Acquisition, Purchasing, etc.) to for acquiring resources, Strategic Alliance contacts for resources from specific partners, etc.

As you begin acquiring resources it is important to keep in mind some lead time items. Depending upon the resource type, the lead time may vary. Some examples include:

- **Financial:** Appropriate funding for the period and work effort expected. This covers the acquisition and "landed costs" of all resource types. Be sure to also plan the timing of the usage of funds. Some budgets are annual, and others are dynamic, this is an important consideration to ensure you will have the funding required when needed.
- **Facilities:** Includes facilities for all resource types. Remote work accommodations may also fall within this area.

- **Human:** Make sure to account time to identify, interview, on-board, and train new people. This can take several weeks.
- **Material:** Allocate time for acquisition, transport, installation, and testing prior to the anticipated use.
- **Technology:** Determine the technology assets required to perform and deliver the work in scope.

Resource allocation follows acquisition. Resource allocation involves more than just assigning people and materials to change activities. It considers the specifics needed (e.g., skills, requirements, capacity, etc.) by the program and delivery teams and the timing required. This also requires a knowledge of the availability of resources. Gauging the timing and meeting the needs of the teams can help reduce costs and increase efficiencies. Be careful of over allocation for human resources. This may create high turnover, thus affecting the quality and timeliness of delivery.

## *Managing, Optimizing, and Releasing Resources*

There are several factors involved in managing, optimizing, and releasing resources. Resource management systems can help in resource forecasting, leveling, monitoring, and releasing.

Resource forecasting is a method of producing the best possible estimates for current and future resource needs. These forecasts are used to help Program Managers, Project Managers and team leads determine whether project activities can be completed based on the number of resources available and the time frame in which they will be needed (Viter, 2022). This consideration must align with the work plans and budget availability. Both program and delivery teams have an important role in ensuring resource management data is up to date in an appropriate system so it can be used to aid planning and allocation.

Resource leveling is a technique used to manage human resource allocation by reviewing constraints and availability. For example, if a resource is assigned to 35 hours of work each week and they work 5/8-hour days, 5 hours may be available for other work. Counter to this is if someone is assigned on multiple tasks that net up to 60 hours and they work a 40-hour week, they are overallocated by 50% and something must change if they are not planning to work 60 hours in that week. If this is seen as a trend overtime, additional resources will be needed for the role they perform.

After a plan is in place, monitoring resources begins. This is a multifaceted process based on the type of resource. Generally, it relates to monitoring resources to determine the value received in terms of efficiency and effectiveness. For material resources, this could be capacity and performance monitoring. For people, various performance factors are considered. Resource optimization may include a periodic review of utilization, throughput, or other relevant measure or metric to determine if the value is received from a specific resource or group of resources.

Resources are added and released from programs and delivery work based on the needs of the initiative. Releasing human resources focuses on releasing the final deliverables to the customer, properly transitioning knowledge (and documentation) to the organization that will handle ongoing support (operations or business areas), closing supplier contracts, releasing in-house resources, and communicating the closure of the project to all stakeholders. For in-house resources, the process should begin a few weeks before the anticipated release date to ensure they are aligned properly with their next assignment. In some cases, the delivery team resources may ultimately support the changes released or they may move on to another program or delivery team.

## Techniques for Agility in Program Resource Management

To achieve agility in resource management a resource management function should be setup at the program level. This function can define standards for metrics and processes to manage different resource types at all levels. Certainly, if standards and processes exist from prior efforts they should be leveraged for the current program and associated change activities. Some considerations to improved team and organizational agility in this practice area are described below. This area is most closely associated with *organizational competency*.

## *Provide opportunities for Citizen Developers*

Provide opportunities for Robotic Process Automation (RPA) or Low/No Code solutions for "citizen developers." These tools provide several opportunities for quality improvement. From one perspective, individual "business users" may develop prototypes using this method that pave the way for their requirements to be more readily understood when larger systems are required.

RPA provides automation capabilities in the hands of end users to reduce the need to engage development teams for certain solutions. Low/No Code development also provides opportunities for individuals to collect and distribute data from multiple sources without human intervention. For example, many areas use multiple spreadsheets and low code tools can help integrate this information and remove redundancies or help identify sources of inconsistent or incorrect data. As a simple example, consider my first name could be stored as Jim, James, or the letter "J" depending on the system (I prefer Jim when talking but always use James when interacting with companies). A citizen developer could use the code to check if the first names agree across systems.

### *Account for and Manage Non-Work Time*

When planning work, consider a 60-70% overall productivity rate for human resources. This number accounts for two key metrics: utilization and productivity. Utilization (aka Availability) is simply the number of hours away over the total number of hours. Meaning, hours away (e.g., PTO, Sick, Training, etc.) should be reduced from the total number of annual hours:

- 160 Hours: Personal time (vacation)
- 80 hours: Sick time
- 60 hours: Training time
- 300 hours / 2080: 1 = 85.57% utilization

Productive time is the amount of time in a day a person is actively working on their assignments. Often this is calculated as hours worked/output produced. Since this isn't always easy to measure, it may be helpful to consider and focus on removing distractors at work that impact productivity. Some of these include non-productive or over attended meetings, being assigned multiple concurrent tasks, interruptions by co-workers stopping by, etc. This can be up to 25% of a person's time. When considering only 85% is available time 75% productive, the net 85% x 75% = 64% productive. Getting a handle of the biggest distractors can make the team more effective individually and collectively.

### *Account for Sourcing Challenges*

Regardless of the market conditions, there are always different types of resources that are in short supply and high demand. These may include physical resources (equipment, etc.) or human resources. By understanding the type of resources that the program may require and identifying and securing multiple sources of those resource pools, the program may experience lowers costs by being able to apply a just-in-time approach and not having resources acquired too far in advance of the need. Or possibly worse, having other resources tied up waiting for a key resource. Factoring in lead time based on availability, manufacturing time, supply chain, or other aspects should be considered when acquiring new or additional resources.

## Consider All Sources for Short-Term Needs

Look thoroughly internally first. A few years ago, I lead a program for a cruise line. We required people who knew their way around a ship's information technology stack and who also understood the protocol when working on ships. We first looked in the offices and found only a few resources, then we considered IT Officers from ships that were going to into drydock (maintenance). By looking at those ships and associated team members, we were able to secure five IT Officers who more than met the requirements and saved us time in both training and recruiting. It also provided them with an income source considering their vessel was unavailable while in drydock (win-win).

## Keep Your Most Valuable Assets and Resources Productive (and Happy)

Finally, it's important to take care of your resources. High turnover can lead to a significant loss in capability and productivity. Keeping your most valuable employees satisfied and productive should be your top priority. To achieve this, it's essential to communicate with them and understand their motivations. This will help you recognize their contributions and keep them engaged in their work. Consider offer training programs, opportunities to attend conference, pay and incentive increases. Other ideas include (Townsend, 2022):

- Don't over-utilize to reduce burnout. Try to limit the number of parallel tasks and your team will perform better.
- Avoid or limit multi-tasking. Multi-tasking sounds efficient, but often results in lower overall productivity.
- Consider the long-term effects of agile practices on people. Over time the continuous quest for speed may either erode quality or fatigue resources.

# Chapter 17:

# Risk Management

Risk Management is at the cornerstone of a program's initiation process. An initial risk assessment is conducted as a part of the business case to determine if the rewards/outcomes expected to be realized

> **Risk Management**
> Involves the process of identifying, assessing, developing mitigation and response plans, and monitoring and responding to risks that arise over the program life cycle.

outweigh the risks of committing resources and performing the work. The risk management process continues iteratively throughout the program delivery lifecycle to ensure that the outcomes are achievable.

As discussed earlier, programs support the delivery of change activities. Change activities generally involve a level of complexity and uncertainty in that the work performed by the delivery teams is unique for that specific instance. Risks and issues can be found at both the delivery team level and at the program level. While delivery teams focus on risks and issues within their purview, the program team helps facilitate the management of those risks, issues and changes that have the potential to impact program outcomes or have a potential significant impact on delivery activity.

An example of a risk that could impact more than one change team may be a supply chain concern. If more than one team is reliant directly (or indirectly) on the timely delivery of a physical product, plans need to be in place to mitigate the impact of that late shipment. These could include contingency plans to source from another vendor, or to provide additional lead time when working with a certain supplier. The program team can help facilitate these mitigation plans and seek alternatives.

## Scope of Program Risk Management

Risks may come from internal or external sources and may arise due to deliberate or unintentional means (Invest Northern Ireland, 2023). Considering this broad scope of potential risks, it may be helpful to break down the potential categories. Patanakul (2008) conducted a literature review to identify common risk categories. His review of eight models did not yield a common definitive list. Lavanya and Malarvizhi (2008) suggested that risks for "project management" fall within four categories: technical, external, organizational, and project management related.

Considering the work of Lavanya and Malarvizhi (2008) and the categories in the eight models reviewed by Patanakul (2008), four categories were selected for program risk management. The categories include:

- **Customer Risks:** Risks arising from internal or external end users (or their representatives [e.g., agents, trade unions, etc.]) of the change activity (project, organizational change, service, solution, other activity, or desired result).
- **Program Management Risks:** Risks identified while performing program governance, strategic alignment, or delivery support activities.
- **Organizational Risks:** Risks associated with (non-program) internal organizations including compliance, finance, human resources, legal, marketing, sales, supply chain, etc.

- **External Risks:** Those risks that come from suppliers, influencers, competitors, etc.

By understanding the source of potential risks and developing appropriate categories, it becomes easier to manage the overall lifecycle. Considering the risk categories described above, the program team should seek those who have the most knowledge about or are closest to the stakeholder communities represented in each respective category to aid in risk management throughout the lifecycle.

## Risk Management Process

The risk management process includes the ongoing identification, assessment (including mitigation and response planning), and overall monitoring of potential or known risks and issues, and subsequent mitigation should the risk be realized. For each area additional information is provided below.

### Risk Identification

There are a multitude of origins of risks and issues in a program. In his 2014 book entitled *Managing Complex Projects and Programs,* Dr. Richard Heaslip defines five types of uncertainty and complexity in programmatic endeavors that include: environmental, organizational, stakeholders, operational, and outcome related. By developing a list with these headings, a brainstorming session can be held with the team to identify specific risks using these categories.

### <u>RICE vs. RAID</u>

Delivery teams often use the acronym of RAID to document and track risks, assumptions, issues, and dependencies. I find the specific inclusion of assumptions and dependencies in the acronym to be redundant. Assumptions and dependencies may or may not lead to risks and, in my opinion, should be regarded the same as other risk types. By focusing on specific risk types (A&D), other risk types may be inadvertently excluded.

Each program practice area should be assessed for risks. Because of this, I created (*a redefined*) risk model (and associated acronym) for Program-level risks, the RICE (Risk / Issue / Commitment / Expectation) log. The RICE log is populated by interrogating risks and issues in the areas described earlier (by Dr. Heaslip and in the program practices areas) against commitments and expectations. The "expectations" type risks are often the least documented, yet *ironically* the most unexpected and detrimental. There are many involved in programs and their expectations can derail the program as much as actual commitments. As such, both commitments and expectations must be documented and tracked – what you said you will do (commitments) and what your stakeholders think you will do (expectations) so not to be blindsided by a risk that becomes a reality.

## Risk format

When documenting risks, I find it helpful to write them out in the following format:

**IF** [Specific risk occurs], **THEN** [ impact to the program or organization], **RESULTING IN** [impact to outcomes].

Using an example from above:

**IF** [the Chief Architect leaves] **THEN** [There will be a gap in having a key resource responsible for technical decisions] **RESULTING IN** [potential delays in the design and sign-off on deliverables].

Using this format, you can see the problem, impact, and result of a risk rather than just saying "There is a risk that the Chief Architect may leave" (which is how I've seen many risks documented).

## *Risk Assessment and Response*

Following the risk identification, the assessment begins with a review of program-level commitments and expectations. Risk assessments can involve complex models and methods to help determine the most pertinent risks to the program. As a pragmatist, I find value in common simple solutions as they are easy to perform and communicate (and share, train, and delegate). One of the most common methods for risk assessment is to develop a scorecard that provides a composite score based on determining the likelihood (probability) of the risk occurring and the impact (severity) if the risk does occur. Based on the composite score, those risks are tracked more closely in subsequent phases (see Figure 25).

Risks that score 1-4 are on the low likelihood or impact scale, they are simply monitored. Risks with scores of 5-12 pose a moderate to major impact to the program or area under consideration (see categories 1-1 in the scope section above). These risks require mitigation plans and need to be actively monitored. Risk in the range above 15 requires both mitigation and response plans (discussed in the next section).

| | | **Impact** | | | | |
|---|---|---|---|---|---|---|
| | | 1 | 2 | 3 | 4 | 5 |
| | | Slight | Minor | Moderate | Major | Catastrophic |
| **Likelihood** | 1 Rare | 1 | 2 | 3 | 4 | 5 |
| | 2 Unlikely | 2 | 4 | 6 | 8 | 10 |
| | 3 Possible | 3 | 6 | 9 | 12 | 15 |
| | 4 Likely | 4 | 8 | 12 | 16 | 20 |
| | 5 Certain | 5 | 10 | 15 | 20 | 25 |

*Figure 25.* A Risk Calculator provides a composite score to help identify risks that may significantly impact to the program.

## *Risk Mitigation and Response Planning*

Risk mitigation planning begins with a review of the risks, the composite scores above, and any other documentation related to the risk. The next step is to determine the best strategy to take for each risk that may include the following:

- **Avoiding:** This can be accomplished by cancelling the program. For example, if the risk of making a profit is deemed unattainable, this may be the strategy, depending upon other factors.
- **Transferring:** The risk may be transferred to an external third-party supplier/provider. This transfer still results in the desired outcome, but possibly at a different cost. All factors need to be weighted to determine the best path.
- **Mitigating:** Includes actions to reduce a risk's likelihood or impact. This could include starting earlier in the process (to reduce a schedule risk), hiring additional qualified people (to reduce a resource risk), or securing new workspace (to reduce a facilities risk).
- **Accepting the risk:** This is often done with risks that score between 1-4 in the matrix above. They

are not likely, or they have low impact, so the team decides to deal with it if factors change (increasing the score) or if it happens.

In any case above there may be residual risk. This is where risk response planning comes into play. Response planning includes documenting strategies should the risks be realized.

### Risk Monitoring and Response

There are several strategies for putting in place controls for monitoring risks to ensure if they do occur, there is both knowledge of their occurrence and plans in place to deal with the impacts. For systems risks, a variety of monitoring and controlling products are available designed to inform operational teams of any problems encountered.

Similarly, on programs there are processes for determining the health of the program and associated risks. Program metrics can provide information relative to the status of outcomes and usage of resources from a data driven perspective. Program risk reviews are often held twice monthly (or another cadence based on the needs of the performing organization) to review those risks in the moderate to high classification.

Risk response (aka issue management) plans must be in place to aid in the return to the program state prior to the risks occurring. By identifying, assessing, and applying the appropriate strategies and actively monitoring risks the impact to the program should be minimized.

## Techniques for Agility in Risk Management

A couple of new concepts were discussed earlier in this section. Risk Management is most closely aligned with the *structural agility* theme for organizational agility. This is due to the speed at which the program team can respond based on planning appropriate mitigation and response plans. Some of the techniques below mirror the earlier section, albeit with additional details:

- **Think Beyond Commitments and Consider Expectations:** The new acronym RICE includes considerations for risks relative to expectations. I find in many of the stakeholder meetings there are undocumented expectations that may or may not become requirements. It is important to capture, categorize and communicate back to the stakeholders the disposition of the item they "expected." A response could be "the steering committee reviewed and has chosen to (or not to) take action on this time."

- **Consider Opportunities When Discussing Risks:** Positive risks are known as opportunities. There may be several opportunities to consider throughout the life of a program. To take advantage of these, there should be a forum for discussion and the risk forum is an appropriate place to hold these conversations. Opportunities may be separate may come about in mitigation discussions.

- **Develop Contingency Plans:** Most guidance (books, papers, etc.) discusses mitigation strategies and response plans but fails to discuss contingency plans. Mitigation plans involve lowering the impact or likelihood of a risk event. Response plans describe specific actions to take if risks occur. Both leave a residual risk and/or unmet outcomes. Contingency planning may help meet both needs. Contingency planning can be proactive in terms of risk mitigation or responsive in terms of risk response.

- **Conduct Risk Walkthroughs vs. Writing Mitigation Plans:** In order to truly understand the impact of the highest risks, a structured walkthrough may be considered to fully develop a plan that accounts not only the obvious paths, but also alternative paths for risk response. There are several tools that can help, like 5-Whys, 5-Ps (provided in this book), Ishikawa diagram mapping (5Ms), or other toolsets. In all cases, the ability to better understand the risk (especially those of highest impact and likelihood) will create better opportunities for mitigation, response, and contingency plans, resulting in better outcomes for the program and sponsoring organization(s).

# Chapter 18:

# Information Management

Programs generate and leverage a large amount of information over time. That information supports decision-making throughout the program

**Information Management**
Includes defining standard processes for the collection, management, storage, safeguarding, and share information used or created by the program.

delivery lifecycle from the initial business case to the final closure of the program. Information is derived from a variety of internal and external sources. It is imperative for interested parties to have access to the most up-to-date and relevant information when needed. To support this requirement the program needs to put in place an information management process and system for the collection, storage, distribution, security, archiving, and deletion of program information.

## Scope of Program Information

In addition to maintaining the repository of information, people supporting this function may be requested to share that information and define the appropriate controls for dissemination and distribution. Figure 26 below presents some common information requirements based on the stakeholder MUSIC category. As a reminder, the categories are M – Members (of the performing organization), U - User Community, S – Suppliers, I – Influencers, and C – Competitors.

| Category | Information Need | Purpose |
|----------|-----------------|---------|
| M U S | Program Intranet and Internet (if applicable) access | To gather role-based program information. |
| M | Program Status information (i.e., Management dashboards, etc.) | To keep appraised of the current state of the program. Role-based information. |
| M | Program / Application lifecycle management repositories | To keep appraised of the current state of the program. |
| M | Process and Standards Libraries | To aid in the informed compliance of program standards and processes. |

| Category | Information Need | Purpose |
|---|---|---|
| M | Quality management guidelines and metrics | To support quality management activities across the lifecycle. |
| M | Program and Team Meeting minutes and actions guidance | To aid in the management and risk reduction for the program. |
| M | Access to Change and Configuration Management repositories. Code repositories. | To ensure processes are consistently followed and role-based access is provided to those who require it. |
| M S | Supplier/Vendor NDAs, contracts, statements of work, statements of understanding, memorandums of understanding, etc. | Role based access to review internal and external agreements to ensure compliance or support necessary changes. |
| M U S | Government or industry regulations | Depending upon the timing the three noted stakeholders will need access to this information. |

| Category | Information Need | **Purpose** |
|---|---|---|
| M S | Risk Management information | Suppliers may be granted some info if they are in a staff augmentation role or have another need to know. |
| M U | Knowledge base articles and product documentation. Decision trees for operational support | For learning and development for both end users and support team members. |
| M | Information regarding influencers | Research on industry trends, laws, and other sources of influence. |
| M | Competitor Information | Solutions and offerings from direct and indirect competitors. |

*Figure 26.* Stakeholders require different information based on their role.

While this is a long list, it is not exhaustive. There are many types of information required based on the specifics of the program. Also note that the delivery teams will also maintain volumes of information and the program should provide guidance and governance over this information to ensure it is both available and appropriately secured. Finally, external communications should not be shared directly from the program without the appropriate vetting with the sponsoring organization.

## Program Information Management Process

Information management includes the infrastructure used to collect, manage, store, and share information. It also consists of the processes and governance to support the abovementioned activities. The goal is to ensure that information is available to those who need it, when they need it and for the express purpose that they need it. The system of systems must consider the sensitivity of information, both physical and electronic, and provide for role-based access (including where the role is a single person). The basic process includes the following steps:

1. **Identify information needs:** Determine the type of information required to support the program. Consider the needs of delivery teams in this assessment.

2. **Collect program information:** This includes creating, gathering existing information, sourcing third party information. This step includes identifying and closing gaps in the information (or information repositories) needed to support the program.

3. **Organize Information:** This is a critical step in the process. Information is only good if people know where to find it and have been provided the appropriate access to it. Providing this access should be a core part of the on-boarding process for new team members. It is important to note that the information does not need to be centralized. In fact, it shouldn't be. It should be available to those who need it where they expect to see it. For example, a program level intranet site should be used to help direct team members to information they need for their specific role. Software developers and architects will need access to code repositories where the Program Manager would not traditionally need access to this resource.

4. **Distribute and actively manage information:** As information is collected the retention period should be understood for that specific asset. When actively managing the information, it is important to ensure

the information is up-to-date, available based on levels of security, and kept only for as long as it is valuable (and in some cases licensed) and disposed as it is no longer needed or valued. Periodic information audits are conducted and as exceptions or deviations are found the team closes those findings.

5. **Information Disposition:** At the end of the information lifecycle, it may be transferred to a new repository as a part of ongoing operational support, additional information needs may also be identified at this time. Based on the needs of the organization, remaining information may be left in the system it was create, archived, or delete. Much of this is dependent upon each individual organization's policies and legal requirements.

As the program continues over time, the process above is iterated for new and existing information types and sources. Having the information available to the right people, at the right time, in the right format can reduce redundancies, rework, and create a positive flow throughout the program lifecycle.

# Techniques for Agility in Information Management

Information is required to support the full lifecycle of programs from inception to closure. Along the way many decisions are supported with the information maintained by the program team. Information management supports all five organizational agility themes. A few opportunities for additional agility in this area are discussed below:

### Provide Transparency and Visibility

Transparency and visibility are core tenants of agility. While supporting this need, consider that does not mean everyone can or should see everything. The information management team should define and maintain role-based access control to program information. Since sometimes your business partners are also your competitors (yes, it's true), it is important to secure information and provide only on a need-to-know basis. With that said, it is also important not to limit information so much that it hinders performance. The right access level should start with more restrictive and as determined more information is required, only then should it become more available. When securing information keep in mind alternate sources of that same information – if people on your team can get it easier elsewhere, they will, and you will be seen as a roadblock. Also ensure ongoing access is provided for those in post program support roles as role-based access is applied.

### *Provide a Comprehensive View of Program Activities*

There are multiple benefits in this area. First and foremost, the visibility across multiple change activities enables the program team to compare work in progress along with new requests to ensure change activities do not conflict with one another and that there is no duplication of effort (Brown, 2020). Another factor is that transparency provides a current view of the state of the change activities, independently and in aggregate. This helps both management and the delivery teams alike. Management may use the current state in their decision making relative to the application of resources. If the change activity is at risk of delay, it may need additional resources to put it back on track. This transparency also supports the delivery team in making a case for additional resources.

### *Maintain and Enhance Program Processes*

The program team often maintains a common suite of processes and practices that can be leveraged by the program and delivery teams as guidance for their respective work. A Program Management Office (PMO) is often used to provide this service. Today, the PMO function may be subsumed into an Agile Center of Excellence (ACE), Scaled Agile Framework (SAFe®) Lean-Agile Center of Excellence (LACE), Agile Practice Office (APO) or some other construct to align with Agile practices. While there are differences between the constructs, there are also many similarities. The key is to assess the needs of the organization and determine the level of support required.

This support requirement may include maintaining common processes/practices, establishing, and defining metrics, supporting tools, providing Agile coaching, providing training, or supporting Agile/Agile @Scale transformation efforts. In the case of a SAFe® LACE communicating business needs, developing implementation plans, and participating in Program Increment (PI) Planning or Inspect and Adapt (I&A) activities may be required (Lai, 2022). By centralizing the function, the organization can realize cost savings through economies of scale by leveraging that supporting organization.

# Chapter 19:

# Learning & Development

The Great Resignation is as much about employees demanding better learning and development as it is about saying no to toxic workplaces (Campbell, 2021). According to Work Institute's 2020 Retention

> **Learning & Development**
> Is more than providing one time training. It includes both supporting the ongoing onboarding and training needs for those joining and serving on the program and providing development opportunities for individual growth.

Report, a lack of career development opportunities was cited as the main reason for employees were leaving their jobs. This underscores the need for learning and development opportunities throughout the organization.

Learning and development (L&D) as a program management practice area is often overlooked or considered as an afterthought. However, it is imperative to provide opportunities in this area for a program to be truly successful. The redefined model has it as a core practice area due to its alignment with the core principle of *Fostering a Culture of Respect and* contribution to organizational agility. Given that the work of a program is unique in that this may be the first time the organization is working to achieve a specific outcome, produce a specific product or accomplish a specific result, the work involved may or may not be familiar to those brought to the team to meet these objectives.

## Scope of Learning & Development

The scope of the learning and development for program teams is a process of upskilling team members through 1) Training on the specific products, services, technologies, etc. that the program is working to integrate, 2) Instruction on standards and processes employed by the program to meet these deliverables, or 3) Education on supporting or soft skills to meet the needs of a position or role one may be placed in. – resulting in a lower attrition rate. The scope of team members involved in L&D events depends upon their specific roles and responsibilities and the events under consideration.

## Learning & Development Process

The L&D needs assessment is first conducted when the program begins and should be continually assessed throughout the life of the program – at a minimum on a quarterly basis. The needs assessment consists of identifying L&D requirements based on the three areas of scope discussed earlier, along with identifying the L&D opportunities already available at the organizational level. The gap (or L&D need) should be assessed with the appropriate organizational team to identify the best way to address that requirement. The program may take ownership considering the unique aspects of the program or the organization will move forward as the requirement is more common across the organization.

Once the types of training and development opportunities are identified. If it is a program-led event, a member of the program team will identify sources of training. The delivery method must consider globally distributed and remote teams, different time zones, language requirements, and different learning methods (e.g., instructor led, self-paced on-line, etc.). Often teams look internally first, however, external sources may prove beneficial as the speed to delivery and total cost may prove to be lower.

Following the selection of the training source(s), the training is coordinated and delivered. It is important to consider all who may benefit from the training based on the type of training provided. I found in the early years of agile (and somewhat today) it was helpful to train the team, executives, customers, and other key stakeholders involved in the process on the method used (e.g., Scrum, Kanban, etc.). In the long run, everyone felt more connected to the program objectives and had a common understanding of the process to achieve the outcomes.

Following the initial delivery of training, it is important to 1) Provide opportunities for ongoing training, and 2) Provide opportunities for feedback. Programs may last many years and while people leave and join overtime, they should not be at a disadvantage for joining a day, week, or longer after the initial training was provided. Feedback is a core concept in organizational agility in supporting ongoing process improvement.

From a development perspective, the Program Manager should work closely with the resources and if applicable, their management to identify opportunities for advancement. This supports the individuals' needs and puts the program in a long-term positive position with a lower rate of attrition.

# Techniques for Agility in Learning & Development

Learning and development budgets do not have to be large to achieve the objectives. There are many opportunities for knowledge sharing in programs to meet these objectives. Paired programming, train the trainer, buddy systems, mentoring, lunch and learns and many other low-cost opportunities exist where the team members share their knowledge to the benefit of all – both those delivering the training and those who receive it. The organizational agility theme supported by this area is *learning and adaptability*. Other areas to consider follow.

### *Provide Development Opportunities*

Based on a review of the roles discussed earlier in chapter 3, there is a potential for the program to require many roles. Considering the organization may already have interested candidates, the right candidate could be placed on the program as a development opportunity. The program also can leverage existing learning and development opportunities and supplement (as required) with the on-the-job training and coaching and mentoring required to help the new program team member more quickly assimilate their new role. Some additional considerations include:

## Align Career Aspirations with Business Needs

Working collaboratively with employees, their management, and others, program opportunities may arise that support the career aspirations of individuals. As program teams are being staffed and sourced, it is important to consider growth opportunities and not just placements. This provides both growth opportunities for those who are seeking this and management opportunities for those who will mentor and support those new managers.

## Link Program L&D with Organizational L&D

As mentioned above, the sponsoring organization may have a full schedule of planned events that can be leveraged to meet the needs of both the organization and specific people on the program. The program team can help by scheduling the training and other meetings at times to reduce double-booking. The program may source training and development opportunities that can be leveraged by others in the organization and open training events up to other teams. Both cases should be considered to take advantage of opportunities either in advance or in parallel of the needs of the organization.

### Train Everyone – Teams, Managers, Customers

As stated earlier, the more who know how things work, the better. Training on the specific products, services, technologies, etc. that the program is working to integrate, or on standards and processes employed by the program to meet these deliverables will in the long run help everyone. This can help bridge the Business/IT Alignment gap by sharing information at a common level that everyone can not only understand but can explain. I often say, I don't need the Nth level details, but I want the opportunity to *speak intelligently about it.* Meaning I'm comfortable with the subject matter and can add to conversations and ideas on how to best leverage it for the business. Additional ideas include supporting cross functional teams and providing replays of training.

## Support Cross Functional Teams

The Program team should emphasize the use of cross-functional teams. Agile teams are typically made up of members with different skill sets and areas of expertise, who work together closely to achieve common goals. This provides a potential informal training and knowledge sharing opportunity to promote instruction within and across teams. The exposure of one team member's responsibilities to others also helps with their knowledge of the overall workload and workflow and provides an opportunity for them to help (with the newly acquired skills) as needed.

## Provide Replay or On-Demand Opportunities

To meet the needs of new team members and geographically dispersed teams, it is important to consider how training will support ongoing needs as it is sourced. It is already difficult for new team members to assimilate into the environment that others have had months (or years) to come up-to-speed. A full on-boarding package should provide a buddy system and appropriate access to training and program information to help new team members. In addition, support for different languages and time zones should always be considered when procuring, scheduling, and delivering training.

# Chapter 20:
# Supporting Practices

Over the past few decades, several other important practices have gained significant attention and adoption. While some of these appear to be associated with and/or focused on software development, their applicability is found in various business and technology pursuits. While there are many that could have been chosen, this section briefly discusses the following based on their potential contributions to enhance program management and to increase organizational agility. These include:

- Systems Thinking
- Design Thinking
- DevOps/DevSecOps

The following sections are intended to provide an overview of the key concepts and features of each and discuss their applicability and contributions to organizational agility. Certainly, there are volumes of information for each related practice if additional study is desired.

## Systems Thinking

When building new or enhancing existing systems (e.g., processes, products, services, etc.) it is essential to consider the "wholes" and interactions between them and not simply the "parts" in isolation. Systems thinking assumes that all processes in an organization are interrelated, and they work together to achieve a common goal (Grimsley, 2022).

In Donella Meadows' 2009 book, *Thinking in Systems: A Primer*, the author defines a system as "a set of related components that work together in a particular environment to perform whatever functions are required to achieve the system's objective." As discussed earlier, programs today (and systems) are Complex Adaptive

Systems, and to fully understand the whole is to also understand the interactions between the components. Components in isolation will behave differently than when the interactions are introduced. This is why in Information Technology we both unit test (test the part) and system integration test (test the whole). However, when testing the whole, the portions that are not technology enabled also need to be considered (i.e., business processes, non-system data flows, etc.).

Systems thinking involves analyzing solutions to consider the interrelationships between and among systems both at current and overtime to define and design appropriate and complete solutions. Several common concepts in systems thinking are provided below (Arnold & Wade, 2015; Acaroglu, 2017; Prasoon, 2020):

- **Recognize interconnectedness:** This is a shift in mindset from linear or circular to identifying an interconnected array of relationships and key connections of the parts of the system. Keeping in mind the definition provided by Donella Meadows earlier.
- **Synthesis:** is a process of reasoning whereby we put dissimilar parts together to gain an

understanding of the whole. This is the opposite of analysis where we break down the components.

- **Emergence:** is the natural outcome of synthesis. When things come together, other outcomes occur. For example, when creating a new systems interaction, there may be additional work that needs to be performed on the interconnected (receiving) side of the system. When only thinking about the primary system this probably wouldn't be considered. And without that interaction, the success of full system could be compromised.

- **Feedback loops:** Some of the interconnections combine to form cause-effect feedback loops. Systems. thinking requires identifying those feedback loops and understanding how they impact system behavior.

- **Causality:** as a concept in systems thinking is about being able to decipher the way things influence each other in a system. Understanding causality leads to a deeper perspective on agency, feedback loops, connections, and relationships, which are all fundamental parts of systems mapping.

- **Systems Mapping:** is a common tool used in systems thinking. "Things" are mapped to help understand how they interconnect, relate, and act in a complex system. These can be used to develop insights and discoveries to describe how potential proposed systems changes impact the "whole" rather than just the constituent "part."

Systems thinking promotes organizational agility at its very core. By understanding the parts and interactions that make up the whole, organizational responsiveness is truly achievable. This not only provides an opportunity to quickly respond to changes but has in place the very core components to sense the need for change through feedback loops resulting in a full understanding of emerging needs.

Understanding the system is critical before you can create the design. Therefore, Systems thinking should generally precede Design Thinking. From a program perspective both tools have significant merit and should be considered prior to any major undertaking. Depending on the method, process, or framework for the overall program, this may have already been built into the planning process.

## Design Thinking

Design thinking, like agility, is not a new concept. Throughout history people have applied a human-centered process to design in the development of many products and solutions. Cognitive scientist and Nobel Prize laureate Herbert A. Simon is credited as the first to mention design as a way of thinking in his 1969 book, *The Sciences of the Artificial* (Dam & Siang, 2022). The recent change for many may be the application of the design focus (in business objectives) to the beginning of the process during the ideation phase, rather than at the end during the customer acceptance phase. Simply stated, the concept is that by bringing in the user early in the process and immersing them in the design process, the product will more closely align with their needs due to uncovering the requirements beyond what may have been stated or documented – the real needs. There is consensus that the design thinking process is comprised of six phases that include (Murtell, 2021; Gibbons, 2016):

- **Empathize:** Conducting research to develop knowledge of what users want. This includes what they do, say think and feel.
- **Define:** By combining and comparing the research from the first step, insights, clarity, focus and definition of the "wicked problem" are better understood. A briefing is developed and shared in the next phase.
- **Ideate:** This is a brainstorming session where creative and "crazy" ideas can be discussed to meet unmet needs. The goal of this session is to converge on a few strongest solution pathways to pursue.
- **Prototype:** This step involves experimentation; transforming ideas into tangible "artifacts." Proposed solutions may be improved and expanded upon, partially or fully redesigned or simply rejected based on the consensus of the team.
- **Test:** The testing phase allows the users to try the solution and provide feedback. The goal is to determine if the solution does indeed meet the users' needs in how they feel, think or perform their work.

- **Implement:** This phase was omitted in some of the readings I went through. Those who know, know only when the end user community adopts and actively uses a solution can it then be deemed beneficial. This is the true test of success.

Design thinking supports both team and organizational agility in focusing on a core value of *customer collaboration* early in the lifecycle. It also follows the agile manifesto principle of "Businesspeople and developers must work together daily throughout the project." Design thinking is not only limited to the work of the delivery teams but must be considered at the program level. How the program is structured, what work is authorized, approved, how work is governed all can benefit from considering this discipline. By supporting this method, the program can experience enhanced product and service value while providing cost effective solutions that more fully meet customer needs.

## DevOps/DevSecOps

DevOps is a combination of practices, tools and processes aimed at enhancing communications and coordination between development (dev) and operations (ops) teams to increase an organization's ability to deliver at a high velocity. DevOps brings with it changes relative to culture, structure, practices, processes, and tools. By doing so, collaboration, speed, scalability, and reliability of the outcomes are positively impacted.

DevOps originally emerged to help break down the long-standing communications barriers (silos) between development and operations teams. DevOps now is used synonymously with continuous integration/continuous delivery (CI/CD) methods that provide a continual delivery flow of software that automates and integrates the processes between software development and IT teams. DevOps practices today have inextricably linked the two formerly separate entities (Development teams and Operations teams) and shortened the development life cycle to provide continuous delivery of high software quality. DevOps practices, like Agility, are not limited to software but due to the CI/CD processes, this has become the most prevalent usage of the term.

DevSecOps (Development, Security, and Operations) arose in response to external hosting arrangements (i.e., cloud computing) and the omnipresent threat of security incidents. DevSecOps expands DevOps to integrate security controls and checkpoints at each stage of the software development lifecycle to ensure the security of software applications.

By integrating the three teams (Dev, Sec, Ops), several benefits are realized. These include collaboration, speed, scalability, security, and reliability (AWS, 2022):

- **Collaboration:** First and foremost, communications and collaboration are at the center of DevOps and agility. By setting a culture of ownership and accountability, development and operations teams collaborate closely by sharing responsibilities and combining their workflows and jointly focusing on process improvements and efficiency gains.
- **Speed:** The teams are self-managed and self-organized and take ownership of the various portions of the lifecycle. By doing so the teams create a cadence and operate at a higher velocity than if handoffs and gate reviews were required.

- **Scalability:** DevOps practices provide for scalability via automation that drives consistency in practices resulting in reduced risk at scale. The usage of Infrastructure as Code helps organizations manage development, testing and production environments in a repeatable and efficient manner.

- **Security:** By integrating security into the DevOps cycle, DevSecOps pulls in Application Security teams early to fortify the development process from a security and vulnerability mitigation perspective (VMWare, 2022).

- **Reliability:** The quality of applications updates and associated infrastructure changes are automated using CI/CD pipelines. By standardizing and automating, organizations can reliably deliver at a more rapid pace. Continuous integration and continuous delivery practices validate changes are tested before being introduced into the production baseline to ensure a continuously positive customer experience. System performance is also managed in real-time via monitoring and logging practices so impacts can be addressed as they are encountered.

While DevOps/DevSecOps are generally practices used by the delivery teams, it is important for the program team to provide resourcing and support as required to these teams so they may be best positioned for success.

# Part V:

# Program Delivery

# Lifecycle &

# Program

# Outcomes

# Part V:

# Program Delivery Lifecycle

# & Outcomes

The Program Delivery Lifecycle includes activities from the Program Governance, Strategic Alignment, and Program Delivery Support Practice areas as described in Parts III and IV of this book. Program Governance and Strategic Alignment are unique in that they are both Core Practice Areas and include practices for programs. Program Delivery support is dynamic in that it itself is a Core Practice Area, however, there are seven (7) core and three (3) supporting practices in this area as described in Part IV.

This section harmonizes the content from the earlier chapters with the three major phases of a program:

Program Initiation, Continuous Delivery, and Program Closure. The intent is to align the high-level activities performed along each time horizon and provide context for both those facilitating and performing the processes. A full list of program practices aligned with the three major phases of a program can be found in Appendix C: Program Practices and Lifecyle Mapping.

# Chapter 21:
# Program Initiation Phase

As described above, program management serves as a crucial link between the portfolios of organizational strategies and services and the associated change activities the program teams' support. By authorizing and chartering a program, the organization realizes significant advantages by supporting the coordination of multiple concurrent change activities rather than the portfolio team having to manage each separately.

Overall, program management strengthens the alignment towards achieving organizational business strategies, ensures better control, and provides more focus towards benefits realization (Brown, 2020) through its support of the delivery teams. As a part of the Program Initiation Phase, two key activities are performed: program authorization and program startup activities.

## Program Authorization

Program authorization includes activities from the strategic alignment and program delivery practices areas. Although some programs seem to be essentially "preapproved" via the strategy development process, it is still important to develop the business

> **_Focus on Delivery_**
> As a Program Manager, be sure not to become over encumbered by activities to start up and run the program and lose sight of the purpose of the program – delivering value to your customer and meeting the goals of the sponsoring organization.

case (which includes the initial budget for resources) to ensure all key stakeholders are "on-the-same-page" regarding a consensus of the value the program is intended to provide. The business case has a justification section that describes the value proposition for the investment. It is this justification that helps garner the support for the formal approval from the Program Sponsor and subsequent funding via the portfolio team.

### *Business Case Development & Approval*

Sometimes business cases are developed and then a Program Manager is selected. I have found probably equally as often a Program Manager is requested to support the development of a business case for a candidate program. This process begins with reviewing the strategic plan or supporting information to derive an understanding of the goals of the program. High level requirements are elicited and documented to describe an initial list of change activities to support the associated strategic goals. A Rough Order of Magnitude (ROM) estimate is then prepared. A ROM estimate is a general estimate of a program's level of effort, duration, resources, and cost often based on analogous estimating where information from similar past work is used to determine the factors above.

If enough information is available, a parametric (bottom-up) estimate can be derived from calculating the costs against the resource requirements. Parametric is generally more accurate (than analogous), however, it requires more information that may not be available at the time of the initial estimate. A contingency percentage is often added to the estimates due to the risks related to uncertainty of the work. This phase often ends with the delivery and subsequent approval of a business case. Once reviewed and approved, the budget is secured, and program startup activities can commence.

## Program Startup

During program startup, many activities are initiated from across the program delivery practice areas. It is important while setting up the program not to lose sight of the need to get to delivery. It is common for programs to be requested to begin delivery work within two weeks (or shorter) of the business case approval. Some programs already have change activities ongoing and they are grouped into a new program for a variety of reasons described earlier in this book. As a Program Manager, be sure not to become over encumbered by activities to startup and run the program and lose sight of the purpose of the program – delivering value to your customer and meeting the strategic goals of the sponsoring organization. But in saying that always consider the impact on your team – a short term orientation may not be sustainable.

The subsections that follow provide a brief description of the activities performed within each of the governance, strategic alignment, and delivery support practice area during program startup. For additional information, please reference the chapter associated with each practice area as described in Parts III and IV.

### Program Governance

Program Governance activities during the initiation phase include defining the governance structure and establishing governance processes to include the forums and events where governance activities are performed. Additional information can be found in Chapter 11 for this area.

### Program Strategic Alignment

Following the approval of the business case from the program authorization phase, the Program Startup activities that include the development of a program charter and roadmap are next performed.

The Program Charter expands upon the information provided in the business case and provides updates as needed to the subsections (See Chapter 12). Portions of the Program Charter (e.g., purpose, benefits, scope, etc.) that are deemed viewable for all team members are often published on the program intranet site. This foundational information is important to share with all team members as it creates a unity of purpose. It also supports the overall alignment of change efforts as team members become self-policing in the selection and prioritization of changes.

The roadmap is initially approved by a program steering committee and subsequently updated consistently during the continuous delivery phase. The roadmap is used as a baseline for additional detail to be placed into the program backlog. The roadmap is generally a higher-level construct than a program backlog and is intended to communicate the major capabilities or milestones the program will deliver in aggregate based on a timeline. For more information see Figure 16 in Chapter 12.

### Program Delivery Activities

Each of the seven delivery support practice areas are initiated during program initiation. Many of the activities are related to planning and setting up the supporting infrastructure for use in the subsequent program delivery phase. The activities include:

- **Communications and Stakeholder Engagement:** Identifying stakeholders (MUSIC), assessing their needs using the Communications Alignment Matrix, and developing Communications Plans for engaging stakeholders.

- **Quality Management:** Develop Quality Management Plan that includes specific metrics for the program. Quality metrics can also be defined at this time.

- **Organizational Change Management:** Defining the requirements for a plan that positively positions the organization to adopt the changes that come out of this program fully.

- **Resource Management:** Resource estimates are detailed in this phase and the baseline budget is updated.

- **Risk Management:** Considering the initial risks were documented in the business case and charter, in this phase the team establishes a process to follow up on these and any newly identified risks.

- **Information Management:** The program team identifies the requirements, repositories, and stewards of information, both developed internally by the program and sourced externally. Initial role-based groupings are developed.

- **Learning and Development:** Considering the vast array of capabilities and levels of expertise, a plan is developed that considers the best value for the program and organization in the early phases of startup and competencies needed to quickly move into the continuous delivery phase.

Although many references (e.g., standards, books, white papers, etc.) define the approval of a program management plan as the timing or milestone signifying the end of the Program Initiation Phase, in this redefined model, this product and milestone does not exist. Specifically, there is no longer a need for a Program Management Plan, only supporting artifacts (i.e., processes, procedures) to provide guidance for the practice areas discussed throughout this book. From experience and to maintain a culture of agility, there is often not formal transition from the program initiation phase to the continuous delivery phase.

The effort of continuous process improvement continues throughout this and the next phase while keeping in mind the foundational elements described in the Program Initiation Phase each have merit, value, provide a strong foundation for the program, and should be completed as close to the beginning of the program as possible so that they may be leveraged by the program, delivery, and operations teams and other key stakeholders. As discussed earlier, getting to the delivery phase quickly is very important, but certainly not at the detriment of properly vetting change activities to ensure they provide the value and align to the organizational strategy as expected.

Program Management Redefined

# Chapter 22:

# Continuous Delivery Phase

Continuous delivery is a multi-functional discipline that supports the continuous alignment and delivery of outcomes across the organization to *provide the right output or outcome, to the right customer, at the right time and at the right price*. Achieving continuous delivery requires significant collaboration and coordination across many internal and external teams. From an internal perspective, there are generally four levels of the organization (i.e., portfolio, program, delivery, and operations teams) that lead to a strategically aligned, continuous, and concurrent flow of delivery across multiple change activities. The extent to which external teams are involved in the process depends on their relative influence and control of the change activities. For example, if the work is being performed directly for an external customer, then they would be embedded in the process at each appropriate level.

## Program Governance Activities

Program Governance activities during this phase include a series of leadership reviews. These events are held to assess the current progress, validate program effectiveness, and support decision-making as required. The reviews are conducted via the forums discussed earlier in this book. This oversight function is held at both the portfolio to program and program to delivery teams (including Ops and supporting teams as appropriate) to ensure the program is meeting the goals for which it was chartered.

## Program Strategic Alignment Activities

Strategic Alignment activities supporting continuous delivery at the program team level support the introduction of new change requests and the continuous prioritization of the existing backlog. Through the strategic alignment process and other interactions with portfolio and delivery teams, the program team gains intelligence and insights that position them to provide cross team coordination. As organizational strategies change, the program team will adjust the priorities in kind. In addition, the prioritization and selection criteria are defined along with guardrails at the program and team levels. The continuous delivery processes presented below are a function of the strategic alignment process at the program level and performed for each delivery team based on their sphere of responsibility relative to the assigned scope.

### *Continuous Delivery Process*

During the Program Initiation Phase, the program team first identifies, plans, and allocates resources work to meet specific program objectives. While the initial opportunities are identified and initiated, this is an ongoing effort throughout the program delivery lifecycle as priorities change and new opportunities emerge. It's important to note that given the intrinsic uncertainty in programs due to various factors, the program team structure at the beginning of the program may change significantly across the lifecycle. This may include adding or removing teams, expanding, or reducing team size, or any other arrangement required to meet the "current" needs of the program at a given point in time.

To facilitate the continuous delivery process, there are generally five major activities that occur. As depicted in Figure 27, a request for a change activity commonly follows the steps that include: Identification, Qualification, Selection, Delivery, and Transition of change activities. Depending upon the method chosen (i.e., Scrum, Enterprise Kanban, SoS, Disciplined Agile® Delivery, etc.), at any step along the way a change may remain in a state or may be moved forward depending upon the number of changes and that change's relative importance.

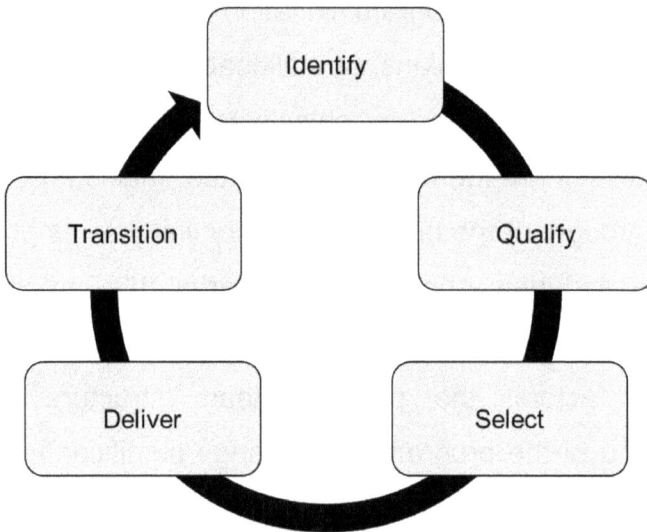

*Figure 27.* The Continuous Delivery Process includes five common steps and potentially involves the collaboration of multiple teams.

Throughout the process above a Program Delivery Manager will facilitate meetings to bring teams together to assess new opportunities, validate priorities of upcoming change activities, coordinate cross team efforts, remove roadblocks, align organizational outputs, and record benefits achieved. *It's important to note that the cycle is continuously occurring at multiple levels both internal and external to the program.* Activities for each phase at each level are defined below.

## Change Activity Identification

The process begins with the identification of changes. New change activities may emerge from any of the following organizational levels for myriad reasons:

- **Enterprise**:  In response to a Political, Economic, Sociological, Technological, Legal, and Environmental stimuli or condition.
- **Portfolio Level:** In response to a competitive product, market condition or single or several customer request(s).
- **Program:** From an architectural perspective as changes are developed and harmonized, new information may arise that requires changes to

foundational elements. Also, from learnings from cross team interactions.

- **Team:** In response to direct customer queries or findings during discovery, development, installation, etc.

- **Separate teams:** Proofs of concept(s), think tanks, and/or hackathons may also be used to generate new ideas and opportunities.


Note: the examples above are illustrative and are not an exhaustive list (by any means). As the change activities are identified, they are added to a backlog with identifying information to include (minimally): a request name, description, requester, and value statement (justification). Depending on the organization, several other fields may be required. I have found the fewer fields requested, the better chance to get what you need. Therefore, it is often best to ask for a little information at first, and more information later.

## Change Activity Qualification

Approval of requests often involve an assessment by either the program team, the delivery team, or the combination of the program and delivery teams. As requests are entered in the identification phase queue, they are then routed to the appropriate area for review and qualification. This process may be facilitated via an automated manner if the requests have enough metadata associated with them or manually, usually by a representative from the program management team.

Qualification entails ensuring the appropriate information is available to make an informed decision whether the change activity request merits being moved forward to the selection and prioritization phase. It may be either simply rejected, additional information may be requested, or the request may be approved at this stage.

## Change Activity Selection & Prioritization

Following the approval during qualification, depending upon the scope of the request, determines the next step. If the requested change is within the guardrails defined for a delivery team, the selection and prioritization may occur at the discretion of this same team. If it requires resources or support beyond a single team or the size, scope and cost are larger than what current teams can easily absorb, then the selection and prioritization will likely be facilitated at the program level. This could be in a scheduled event (e.g., Program Management Review, Program Increment Meeting, etc.) or if deemed of high enough priority, the program may convene a special review board to determine the next steps.

## Change Activity Delivery

As the change comes up in priority and it is actively worked upon, the next logical step is delivery. While delivery is a delivery team responsibility, the program team still has a responsibility for governance (i.e., oversee the delivery, etc.), alignment (e.g., to ensure the change activities continues to evolve toward the strategic goals) and delivery support (e.g., provide funding and resources for cross-team collaboration, etc.). The delivery teams often still "own" support for a short "pretransition" period (aka Warranty Period, Transition Support Period, Hyper Care, etc.). During this period, issues (if encountered) are addressed and closed.

## Change Activity Transition

Finally, after the warranty period, and when the Operations team deems the change activity stable, then they "sign off" on the change and take over the responsibility for ongoing support.

Based on the method selected, some of the detailed information presented above may change; however, the steps above are generally common to most methods in which I've been involved.

# Program Delivery Support Activities

Throughout the continuous delivery process, each of the delivery support practice areas continue to provide support throughout the continuous delivery phase. The activities include:

- **Stakeholder Communications**: Communications are shared with stakeholders via various methods as described earlier. The effectiveness of communications is assessed, and changes are implemented as required.
- **Quality Management**: Reviews are conducted, and Quality Management methods are applied using

appropriate metrics (KPIs, KRA, OKRs, etc.) dependent upon the area under consideration.

- **Organizational Change Management**: As change activities are defined, developed, and delivered, corresponding OCM activities are planned and implemented along with the changes as they are delivered.

- **Resource Management**: Resources (People, Material, Information Management, Financial) are managed throughout the lifecycle. Budgets are maintained and reviewed (min. Monthly). As new changes are proposed, estimates, sourcing and new funding requests are submitted, reviewed, and dispositioned (i.e., partially/fully approved, denied, etc.) as appropriate.

- **Risk Management**: The RICE log is maintained, and activities continue to monitor, mitigate, manage issues, or close risk entries.

- **Information Management**: The program team maintains information, captures metrics, and provides self-service (i.e., dashboards or Intranet information resources) or provides support for custom information requests.

- **Learning and Development**: The team sources and deliver training based on the initial needs assessment in the Initiation Phase and on updates that have been subsequently applied. The program also helps support development activities as appropriate.

As program changes are completed, knowledge is transferred then ownership and support are transitioned. This is an ongoing activity for the bulk of the program. The information created throughout the process should continue to be accessible. As new changes are approved, it's important to leverage both the information that is formally documented and the knowledge of the team members. This information can be used for estimating funding, resource needs, and time estimating for subsequent related or similar work.

Program Management Redefined

# Chapter 23:
# Program Closure Phase

Shortly in advance of the transition of the final change activities to the appropriate operational support teams, program closure activities commence. Like the change from Program

> **Program Closure**
> Must first consider the transition of people to new roles that align with their goals while formally transitioning the change activities, knowledge capital to provide the best opportunity for success.

Initiation to Continuous Delivery, there is a gradual progression to the Program Closure phase. Before closing out a program, the Program Manager must receive approval from the Program Sponsor. As a part of the formal closure, it's important to ensure that the benefits attained are documented, all remaining backlog items and program support activities are properly transitioned to the appropriate steward (e.g., Operations team, potentially a new or existing program, etc.), and the stakeholders have been appraised of the intent to close out the program.

## Program Closure Activities

A review of each practice area should be conducted to ensure that the work performed has either been completed or transferred to the appropriate steward for any required sustainment activities. Some of the final activities to close out a program include the following:

- **Program Governance:** A formal closure review is held with key stakeholders to 1) ensure the program met its objectives and should be closed and if #1 is yes, then 2) share the final outcomes of the program, successes, and lessons learned.
- **Strategic Alignment:** Validate that benefits were indeed achieved, and sustainment activities are performed or planned for remaining work.
- **Communications & Stakeholder Engagement:** Provide final communications to close out the program. Be sure to laud the work of the teams.
- **Quality Management:** Transition any quality management efforts to an appropriate ongoing steward organization.

- **Organizational Change Management:** Validate transition and sustainment activities are in place.
- **Resource Management:** Release resources and close or transition contracts.
- **Risk Management:** Disposition and transition residual or remaining risks.
- **Information Management:** Archiving and final dispositioning of information. Contribute to Process Asset Libraries, Lessons Learned, etc.
- **Learning and Development:** Transition training to the appropriate ongoing steward. Work with management on new opportunities to transition existing internal people.

Once the activities above are complete, along with any specific activities required for your organization, the program can be closed. One important note: Please be sure to properly transition the people. I've seen this done well, and less so. "Availability is not a core skill," meaning, don't send people where there are openings if it is not a good fit. People should, whenever possible, be aligned with their interests for their next opportunity.

# Chapter 24:

# Program Outcomes

Program outcomes represent the cumulative results, benefits, or effects provided by the program that were achieved. Program benefits are initially defined when the program is chartered and

> **Program Outcomes**
> Include cumulative results, benefits, or effects provided by the program that were achieved. These include both those that were defined at the onset and those ancillary benefits achieve along the way.

updated to reflect the desired business results over time as the program continues. While program benefits and outcomes are typically specified in advance of the authorization of change activities, ancillary benefits may also be achieved during the delivery of the primary benefit. For example, if the goal is to produce a software feature that has never been built before (by anyone), the benefit may be the goal (software feature), but ancillary benefits may include a patentable solution that can serve as a differentiator for the organization. Another can be the methods or knowledge capital attained by the team in developing this feature that paves the way to produce other new (never been done before) features even faster.

In general, the change activities chartered by the program produce the primary benefits, however, the program can provide additional benefits by coordinating cross team activities that result in faster delivery and fewer blockers. As a part of the strategic alignment process, the program endeavors to produce benefits that provide a positive impact or value to a group of stakeholders. Both outcomes and benefits are typically specified in advance of a change activity's authorization as a part of the business case and are used to measure its success or effectiveness.

## Measures of Program Success

So how do you know if you're successful? The success criteria, where appropriate, should describe both the benefit to the organization and the customer.

## Organizational Benefits

The benefit to the organization can be measured by the net effect the program provided in terms of Return on Investment (ROI). ROI calculates the financial benefit achieved against the investment costs. Goal achievement type measures consider the success of attaining specific goals that were sought at the on-set of a change activity within the program. These may be represented by Objectives and Key Results (OKR), Key Performance Indicators, or Key Results Areas. Each of these is a measure of performance against a stated goal.

## Customer Success

A common customer satisfaction measure is Net Promoter Score (NPS). NPS is a metric derived from customer responses to questionnaires intended to gauge their satisfaction related to the outcomes or interactions with the teams. Beyond NPS, for consulting organizations, you can gauge customer satisfaction by additional contracts, the level of teaming and involvement in meeting strategic goals, and the length of time the contract organization has held a business relationship.

### *Additional Success Measures*

Measures may also include the individual or cumulative net value provided by the specific change activities within the program based on common quality, performance, efficiency, or value measures or metrics. Figure 28 provides several examples.

| Efficiency Measures | Value Measures | Quality Measures |
|---|---|---|
| • Network speed<br>• First contact resolution (FCR)<br>• IT hours spent on projects<br>• Time to resolution<br>• Accuracy<br>• On time, on budget<br>• Transactions per second<br>• Defect removal<br>• Correct routing<br>• Automation<br>• Appropriate prioritization<br>• Maximum duration of | • Customer Satisfaction<br>• Saved time<br>• Productivity<br>• Business impact<br>• Correlation to business needs<br>• WIIFM (What's in it for me?)<br>• Accuracy<br>• Trending (Top types and Priority<br>• Cost per contact to business | • Baseline impact<br>• System performance monitoring<br>• Incident monitoring<br>• Knowledge monitoring<br>• Quality Index<br>• Core system availability<br>• Coaching<br>• Alignment with goals<br>• Proper sense of urgency<br>• Customer service skills |

| outage<br>• Number of core<br>  system outages<br>• Reliability<br>• Mean time to<br>  repair | | • SLA/OLA<br>  compliance<br>• Service review<br>  meetings and<br>  improvement<br>  plans |
|---|---|---|

*Figure 28* Common efficiency, value, and quality measures

may be used to determine the individual or net impact of change activities on program outcomes (Bruno, 2016).

## Closing Thoughts on Program Success

As stated at the beginning of the book: "No two programs are alike. Each has its own purpose, goals, and objectives." The key is to capture those goals in the beginning of the program and work to pursue them until they are achieved, or other, higher-priority goals are determined. Along the way determining and measuring what matters to the stakeholders will result in a successful venture. But, most importantly, listen to and take care of the people along the way and in that you will be successful.

# Part VI: Appendices

# Part VI:

# Appendices

This section includes four appendices to provide more information in the areas discussed earlier and include:

- **Appendix A: Key Terms and Definitions** – This book contains acronyms, industry terms, and other terminology (i.e., jargon) that may not be familiar to the full audience who may read this book. This section has been created to help bridge this gap as appropriate.

- **Appendix B: Program Practices and Lifecycle Mapping** – A table is provided that describes the tasks in the three phases across the nine practice areas.

- **Appendix C: Organizational Agility Questionnaire** – Dr. Worley was very gracious in providing not only permission (within the book), but he also provided a public link to the survey. I recommend you buy the book as it provides much more information and context than I provided here.

- **Appendix D: References** – Many books, articles, and other publications were sourced to provide content or supporting information throughout this book. They are all listed in this appendix.

- **Appendix E: Index** – Select entries were selected to ease navigation.

# Appendix A: Key Terms and Definitions

# Appendix A:
# Key Terms and Definitions

Several terms, acronyms and abbreviations are used throughout this book. This section provides the definitions for each presented. Where applicable, citations are provided below.

**Agile@Scale Methods** (also Large Scale Agile or Scaling Agile Methods) – Methods to expand Agile teams to support larger team size, geographical distribution, regulatory compliance, organizational distribution, technical complexity, domain complexity, organizational complexity, and enterprise discipline (Ambler, 2010).

**Agile Methods** – Methodologies to provide continuous delivery of valuable software (Fowler & Highsmith, 2001).

**Agile Release Train (ART)** – "A long-lived team of Agile teams, which, along with other stakeholders, incrementally develops, delivers, and where applicable operates, one or more solutions in a value stream" (Scaled Agile Inc., 2023a).

**Burn Up Chart** – "A Burn Up Chart is a visual diagram commonly used on Agile projects to help measure progress. Agile Burn Up Charts allow Project Managers and teams to quickly see how their workload is progressing and whether project completion is on schedule" (Everett, 2020).

**Change Activity** – Change Activities may include process changes, new and enhanced products, projects, organizational change activities, services, solutions, other activities, or desired results associated with that program based on the specific needs of the performing organization.

**Delivery Teams** – Are cross functional and semi-autonomous. Cross functional in that the team is formed with the appropriate expertise to perform the assigned change activities. Semi-autonomous because they are directly responsible for the delivery of their assigned change activities.

**DevOps** – "DevOps (development and operations) is an enterprise software development phrase used to mean a type of agile relationship between development and IT operations. The goal of DevOps is to change and improve the relationship by advocating better communication and collaboration between these two business units" (Beal, 2013). While originally used for software the concept is applicable to any change activity that will be transitioned from a delivery team to an operations team.

**Disciplined Agile® Delivery (DAD)** – Disciplined Agile® Delivery (DAD) is a people-first, learning-oriented hybrid agile approach to IT solution delivery. DAD addresses all aspects of the full delivery life cycle, supporting multiple ways of working (WoW) that can be tailored for the context that you face. DAD encompasses all aspects of agile software development in a robust, pragmatic, and governable manner (PMI, 2023a).

**DSDM** – DSDM is an Agile method that focuses on the full project lifecycle, DSDM (formally known as Dynamic System Development Method) was created in 1994, after project managers using RAD (Rapid Application Development) sought more governance and discipline to this new iterative way of working (Agile Business Consortium, 2023).

**Effectiveness** – See Organizational Effectiveness.

**Kanban** – Kanban is a visual system used to manage and keep track of work as it moves through a process. The word Kanban is Japanese and roughly translated means "card you can see."

**Large Scale Agile Methods** – See Agile@Scale Methods

**Large Scale Scrum (LeSS)** – Large Scale Scrum (LeSS) uses the principles of Scrum in a large-scale context where multiple teams collaborate to produce one shippable product. There are two types of Large Scale Scrum; Basic LeSS and LeSS Huge. Basic LeSS is similar to single-team Scrum and works best for two to eight teams (between 10 and 50 employees). LeSS Huge focuses on big projects where more than eight Scrum teams (anywhere over 50 employees) work together to deliver a single shippable product (Product HQ, 2023).

**Nexus Framework** – Nexus is an Agile framework that is used in a scaled agile project where there are approximately three to nine Scrum development teams, each made up of five to nine members, and there is one common product backlog used by all of the teams (Agilest, 2023).

**Open Systems** – An Organization Design construct characterized by considering the interdependent nature of systems being interconnected and mutually influential.

**Organizational Agility** – "the ability to detect and respond to opportunities and threats with ease, speed, and dexterity" (Tallon & Pinsonneault, 2011, p. 464).

**Organizational Effectiveness** – The extent to which an organization, using certain resources, efficiently fulfils its objectives without depleting its resources and without placing undue strain on its members and/or society (Manzoor, 2011).

**Organizational Performance** – The Baldrige National Quality Program defines an "organization's performance and improvement in its key business areas: customer satisfaction, financial and marketplace performance, workforce, product/service, operational effectiveness, and leadership. The category also examines how the organization performs relative to competitors" (Hook, Burge, & Bagg, 2017, p. 7).

**Organizational Design Theory** – The study of how organizations function and how they affect and are affected by the environment in which they operate (Jones, 2013).

**PMI** – The Project Management Institute.

**Portfolio Management** – is an organizational function that prioritizes and allocates resources (e.g., financial, facilities, human, material, technology, etc.) to change activities by "investing" in initiatives that align with organizational strategies.

**Product Manager** – The Product Manager role is strategic in that they focus on the product vision, competition, market, and organizational strategic objectives.

**Product Owner** – "The Product Owner (PO) is a member of the Agile Team responsible for defining Stories and prioritizing the Team Backlog to streamline the execution of program priorities while maintaining the conceptual and technical integrity of the Features or components for the team" (Scaled Agile Inc., 2023c).

**Program Change Activities** – Change activities may take the form of business process changes, new and enhanced products, projects, operations, organizational change activities, services, solutions, and other activities associated with that program based on the specific needs of the performing organization.

**Program Delivery Coordination Meeting** – See Scrum of Scrums

**Program Increment** – "A Program Increment (PI) is a timeboxed planning interval during which an Agile

Release Train plans and delivers incremental value in the form of working, tested software and systems. PIs are typically 8 – 12 weeks long" (Scaled Agile Inc., 2023d).

**Program Management** – Is an organizational entity that provides a governance and delivery support function that is used to align and coordinate a group of change activities performed by delivery teams that provide benefits to stakeholders.

**Program Manager** – A Program Manager has the overall responsibility for leading the program. They have three primary responsibilities for Governance, Strategic Alignment and Delivery Support. They work closely with the Program Sponsor, Organizational Change Manager(s), Product Manager(s), and Chief Architect(s) to define the program scope, continuously reprioritize work, and they establish the delivery teams and coordinate the activities amongst the same teams (Delivery Team Leads [Scrum Masters, Project Managers, etc.]) and operations team members.

**Project** – A project is "a temporary endeavor undertaken to create a unique product, service or result" (PMI, 2013, p. 3).

**Project Management** – Project Management is "the application of knowledge, skills, tools, and techniques to project activities to meet project requirements" (Project Management Institute, 2013, p. 5).

**Program Quality** – "The degree to which a set of inherent characteristics fulfills requirements" (Project Management Institute, 2019, p. 718).

**Release Train Engineer (RTE)** – A role in the Scaled Agile Framework. The Release Train Engineer (RTE) is a servant leader and coach for the Agile Release Train (ART). The RTE's major responsibilities are to facilitate the ART events and processes and assist the teams in delivering value. RTEs communicate with stakeholders, escalate impediments, help manage risk, and drive relentless improvement. (Scaled Agile Inc., 2023e).

**Recipes for Agile Governance in the Enterprise (RAGE)** – Kevin Thompson of cPrime documented Recipes for Agile Governance in the Enterprise in a 2013 paper. (RAGE). Agile Program Management according to the RAGE model relies on key Ceremonies such as the Release Planning meeting, Team Scrum-of-Scrums meetings, Product Owner Scrum-of-Scrums meetings, Release Backlog Grooming meetings, Release Review, and Release Retrospective meetings. It also defines Area Product Owner roles and Program Manager roles, and measures progress with Burn Up Charts (cPrime, 2016).

**SAFe® – Scaled Agile Framework** – "The Scaled Agile Framework encompasses a set of principles, processes and best practices that helps larger organizations adopt Agile methodologies, such as Lean and Scrum, to develop and deliver high-quality products and services faster" (Alexander, 2019).

**SAFe® Lean-Agile Principles** – SAFe is based on ten immutable, underlying Lean-Agile principles. These tenets and economic concepts inspire and inform the roles and practices of SAFe (Scaled Agile Inc., 2023b).

**Scaling Agile Methods** – See Agile@Scale Methods.

**Scaling Agile @ Spotify** – See Spotify Framework.

**Scrum** – A framework within which people can address complex adaptive problems, while productively and creatively delivering products of the highest possible value (Sutherland & Schwaber, 2017).

**Scrum Master** – In any given situation, a Scrum Master utilizes their important soft skills to act as a Servant Leader, Facilitator, Coach, Manager, Mentor, Teacher, Impediment Remover or Change Agent, depending on the situation at hand (Overeem, 2017).

**Scrum of Scrums** – A technique to scale Scrum up to large groups (over a dozen people), consisting of dividing the groups into Agile teams of 5-10. Each daily scrum within a sub-team ends by designating one member as "ambassador" to participate in a daily meeting with ambassadors from other teams, called the Scrum of Scrums (AgileAlliance.org, 2023).

**Software Development** – Software development is an iterative logical process that aims to create a computer coded or programmed software to address a unique business or personal objective, goal, or process (Technopedia.com, n.d.).

**Spotify Framework** – The Spotify model is a people-driven, autonomous approach for scaling agile that emphasizes the importance of culture and network. It has helped Spotify and other organizations increase innovation and productivity by focusing on autonomy, communication, accountability, and quality (Atlassian, 2023).

**Stakeholders** – Include internal and external individuals, groups, or organizations who have an interest in the program who may directly or indirectly, positively, or negatively impact the program outcomes.

**Story Points** – A "Story Point is a measure for relatively expressing the overall size of a user story or a feature. The value of the Story Point is dependent on the development complexity, effort involved, and the inherent risk" (Coelho, & Basu, 2012).

**Strategic Alignment** – The "degree to which the information technology [or change activity] mission, objectives, and plans support and are supported by the business mission, objectives, and plans" (Reich & Benbaset, 2000, p. 82).

**Strategic Objectives** – The "aims or responses that your organization articulates to address major change or improvement, competitiveness or social issues, and business advantages" (Scott, 2016).

**Technical Debt** – Technical debt (TD) refers to the practice of relying on temporary easy-to-implement solutions to achieve short-term results at the expense of efficiency in the long run. The metaphor coined by Ward Cunningham in 2009, author of Agile Manifesto, for describing the impact of accruing tech issues (Tkachuk, 2021).

**User Story** – Is a short, simple description of a feature told from the perspective of the person who desires the new capability, usually a user or customer of the system. (Cohn, 2022). User stories typically follow a simple template: As a < type of user >, I want < some goal > so that < some reason >.

**Velocity** – "Velocity is a measure of the team's progress rate. It is calculated by adding all the Story Points assigned to each user story completed by the team in the current iteration" (Coelho, & Basu, 2012).

**Waterfall Method** – The Waterfall model is a sequential software development process model that follows defined phases using the software development life cycle's (SDLC) common steps. The Waterfall model enforces moving to the next phase only after completion of the previous phase (Tools QA, 2021).

# Appendix B: Program Practices & Lifecycle Mapping

# Appendix B:
# Program Practices and
# Lifecycle Mapping

| Program Initiation | Continuous Delivery | Program Closure |
|---|---|---|
| **Program Governance** | | |
| • Define Governance Structure. <br> • Establish Governance Processes. <br> • Determine Governance Forums. | • Hold Leadership Reviews. <br> • Validate effectiveness, change as required. | • Hold formal closure review. |
| **Strategic Alignment** | | |
| • Develop Business Case <br> • Develop Program Charter. <br> • Develop Program Roadmap. | • Maintain 360 view. <br> • Continuous prioritization of backlog. <br> • Coordination of Delivery Teams. <br> • Prioritize and select. | • Validate and document benefits. <br> • Ensure remain activities are transitioned for ongoing support. |

| Program Initiation | Continuous Delivery | Program Closure |
|---|---|---|
| **Communications & Stakeholder Engagement** | | |
| • Identify Stakeholders MUSIC.<br>• Assess Stakeholder Needs.<br>• Develop Communications and Stakeholder Engagement Plan. | • Maintain communications, update as required. | • Provide final communications to closeout program. |
| **Quality Management** | | |
| • Develop Quality Mgmt. Plan.<br>• Define Program Metrics. | • Review Quality using appropriate metrics (KPIs, KRA, OKRs, etc.). | • Transition to ongoing steward. |
| **Organizational Change Management** | | |
| • Prepare for Organizational Change. | • Conduct OCM activities. | • Validate transition and sustainment activities are in place. |
| **Resource Management** | | |
| • Estimate Resource Requirements.<br>• Define baseline budget. | • Manage Resources (e.g., financial, facilities, human, material, technology, etc.).<br>• Maintain Budget (min. Monthly).<br>• Estimate and | • Release resources, close contracts. |

| Program Initiation | Continuous Delivery | Program Closure |
|---|---|---|
| | source new funding for new opportunities. | |

### Risk Management

| | | |
|---|---|---|
| • Develop Risk Mgmt. Plan.<br>• Identify initial Risks/Issues. | • Maintain RICE log (Monitor/Mitigate/Close). | • Disposition and transition residual or remaining risks. |

### Information Management

| | | |
|---|---|---|
| • Identify Information Needs.<br>• Define repositories by type. | • Maintain program info.<br>• Capture and provide. Metrics/ Dashboard or Intranet Reporting. | • Transition to ongoing steward. |

### Learning and Development

| | | |
|---|---|---|
| • Develop Training and Development Plan. | • Source and deliver training.<br>• Support development activities, | • Transition to ongoing steward. |

# Appendix C: Organizational Agility Questionnaire

# Appendix C: Organizational Agility Questionnaire

| Q. | Our organization… | Strongly Disagree | Disagree Somewhat | Agree Somewhat | Strongly Agree |
|---|---|---|---|---|---|
| 1 | …has a unifying purpose or mission other than profitability and growth. | 1 | 2 | 3 | 4 |
| 2 | …spends a lot of time thinking about the future. | 1 | 2 | 3 | 4 |
| 3 | …encourages innovation | 1 | 2 | 3 | 4 |
| 4 | …considers the ability to change a strength of the organization. | 1 | 2 | 3 | 4 |

| Q. | Our organization… | Strongly Disagree | Disagree Somewhat | Agree Somewhat | Strongly Agree |
|---|---|---|---|---|---|
| 5 | …develops strategies with flexibility in mind. | 1 | 2 | 3 | 4 |
| 6 | …puts as many employees as possible in contact with the external environment, especially with customers. | 1 | 2 | 3 | 4 |
| 7 | …has enough budget "slack" so that people can develop new products or better ways of working together. | 1 | 2 | 3 | 4 |
| 8 | …has a well-developed change capability. | 1 | 2 | 3 | 4 |
| 9 | …has a culture that embraces change as normal. | 1 | 2 | 3 | 4 |

# Organizational Agility Questionnaire

| Q. | Our organization… | Strongly Disagree | Disagree Somewhat | Agree Somewhat | Strongly Agree |
|---|---|---|---|---|---|
| 10 | … allows information to flow freely from the outside to units and groups where it is most valuable. | 1 | 2 | 3 | 4 |
| 11 | …has flexible budgets that respond to marketplace changes. | 1 | 2 | 3 | 4 |
| 12 | …rewards seniority more than performance. (Note: reverse scoring) | 4 | 3 | 2 | 1 |
| 13 | …has core values that reflect a change-ready organization. | 1 | 2 | 3 | 4 |
| 14 | …shares financial and business strategy information with all employees. | 1 | 2 | 3 | 4 |

| Q. | Our organization… | Strongly Disagree | Disagree Somewhat | Agree Somewhat | Strongly Agree |
|---|---|---|---|---|---|
| 15 | …is capable of shifting its structure quickly to address new opportunities. | 1 | 2 | 3 | 4 |
| 16 | …pays for skills and knowledge that contribute to performance. | 1 | 2 | 3 | 4 |
| 17 | …regularly reviews learnings from change efforts. | 1 | 2 | 3 | 4 |
| 18 | …has formal mechanisms to connect senior management with people at all levels of the organization. | 1 | 2 | 3 | 4 |
| 19 | …encourages managers to develop the leadership skills of their direct reports. | 1 | 2 | 3 | 4 |

**Scoring Instructions**

To derive a score for each criterion, calculate the following (Center for Effective Organizations [n.d.]):

- Dynamic Strategy/Strategizing
  - Add Q1 + Q5 + Q9 + Q13 and divide by 4.
- Perceiving
  - Add Q2 + Q6 + Q10 + Q14 + Q18 and divide by 5.
- Testing
  - Add Q3 + Q7 + Q11 + Q15 + Q17 and divide by 5.
- Implementing
  - Add Q4 + Q8 + **Q12** + Q16 + Q19 and divide by 5.
  - Q12 is inversely coded - Recalculate score for question 12 as:
    - Score = 5 – x (where x is input).
- Total Score
  - Add the results of the scores above and divide by 4.

For more information, please refer to: Worley, Christopher G., Thomas D. Williams, and Edward E. Lawler III. *Assessing Organization Agility: Creating Diagnostic Profiles to Guide Transformation.* John Wiley & Sons, 2014.

# Appendix D:
# References

# Appendix D: References

18F. 2017. "Agile is Something You Are." Retrieved from https://agile.18f.gov/. *Agile Principles and 18F Practices*. U.S. General Services Administration.

Acaroglu, Leyla. 2017. "Tools for Systems Thinkers: The 6 Fundamental Concepts of Systems Thinking." *Medium.* Retrieved from https://medium.com/disruptive-design/tools-for-systems-thinkers-the-6-fundamental-concepts-of-systems-thinking-379cdac3dc6a.

Agile Alliance. 2022. "About Agile Alliance. What is Agile Alliance and What Does it Do?" Retrieved from https://www.agilealliance.org/the-alliance/.

Agile Alliance. 2022. "Kanban." Retrieved from

https://www.agilealliance.org/glossary/kanban/.

Agile Alliance. 2023. "Scrum of Scrums." Retrieved from https://www.agilealliance.org/glossary/scrum-of-scrums/.

Agile Business Consortium. 2023. "What is DSDM?" Retrieved from https://www.agilebusiness.org/page/whatisdsdm.

Agilest. 2023. "Nexus Framework." Retrieved from https://www.agilest.org/scaled-agile/nexus-framework/.

Alexander, Maggie. 2019. "What is SAFe? The Scaled Agile Framework Explained." CIO. Retrieved from https://www.cio.com/article/3434530/what-is-safe-the-scaled-agile-framework-explained.html.

Alzoubi, Ahmad, Eyad Haider, Firas J. Al-otoum, and Amro K.F. Albatainh. 2011. "Factors Affecting Organization Agility on Product Development." *International Journal of Research and Reviews in Applied Sciences* 9, no. 3 (2011): 503-515.

Amazon Web Services. 2022. "What is DevOps?"

Retrieved                                    from https://aws.amazon.com/devops/what-is-devops/.

Ambler, Scott W. 2010. "Scaling Agile: An Executive Guide." *IBM Agility at Scale*.

Ambler, Scott W., and Mark Lines. 2012. *Disciplined Agile Delivery: A Practitioner's Guide to Agile Software Delivery in the Enterprise*. IBM Press.

Ambler, Scott W. 2019. "The Principles Behind Disciplined Agile." Retrieved from https://www.projectmanagement.com/blog/blogPosti ngView.cfm?blogPostingID=56589&thisPageURL=/ blog-post/56589/The-Principles-Behind-Disciplined-Agile.

American Society for Quality. 2022. "Failure Mode and Effects Analysis (FMEA)." Retrieved from https://asq.org/quality-resources/fmea.

Arnold, R. D., and Wade, J. P. 2015. "A Definition of Systems Thinking: A Systems Approach." *Procedia Computer Science* 44:669–678. Retrieved from https://doi.org/10.1016/j.procs.2015.03.050.

Atlassian. 2023. "Discover the Spotify Model." Accessed March 6, 2023. Retrieved from https://www.atlassian.com/agile/agile-at-scale/spotify#:~:text=What%20is%20the%20Spotify%20model,communication%2C%20accountability%2C%20and%20quality.

Axelos. 2020. *Managing Successful Programmes*. 5th ed. The Stationery Office.

Beal, V. 2013. "DevOps – Development and Operations." *Webopedia*. Retrieved from https://www.webopedia.com/definitions/devops-development-operations/.

Beezley, J. 2018. "Guiding principles offer direction, add clarity for large HIT projects." Healthcare IT Leaders. Retrieved from https://www.healthcareitleaders.com/blog/guiding-principles-offer-direction-add-clarity-large-hit-projects/#:~:text=Guiding%20principles%20are%20simple%20rules,quickly%20and%20with%20greater%20autonomy.

Brown, L. 2020. "Key benefits of Program Management."

Invensis Learning. Retrieved from https://www.invensislearning.com/blog/benefits-program-management/.

Bruno, A. 2016. "Measuring Operational Efficiency and Value: Use Metrics to Tell the Business Story." HDI. Retrieved from https://www.thinkhdi.com/library/supportworld/2016/measuring-operational-efficiency-value.aspx.

Burke, W. W. 2017. *Organization Change: Theory and Practice*. Sage Publications.

Burke, W. W., & Litwin, G. H. 1992. "A causal model of organizational performance and change." *Journal of Management*, 18(3), 523-545.

Brown, L. 2022. "Why program management is essential for an organization." Invensis Learning. Retrieved from https://www.invensislearning.com/blog/why-program-management-is-essential-for-an-organization/.

Byrn, D. 2022. "What are the five principles of corporate governance?" The Corporate Governance Institute. Retrieved from

https://www.thecorporategovernanceinstitute.com/in
sights/lexicon/what-are-the-five-principles-of-
corporate-governance/.

Campbell, F. 2021. "A comprehensive guide to learning
and development in the UK." 360Learning.
Retrieved from https://360learning.com/blog/uk-
learning-and-development/.

CB Insights. 2021. "The top 12 reasons startups fail."
Retrieved                                from
https://www.cbinsights.com/research/report/startup-
failure-reasons-top/.

Center for Effective Organizations. n.d. "Short survey:
Organizational Agility Profiler Survey." University of
Southern California. Retrieved on February 8, 2023,
from                            https://ceo.usc.edu/wp-
content/uploads/2020/02/Short_Survey_Agility_Profi
ler_web.pdf.

Chan, S. 2001. "Complex adaptive systems." In ESD. 83
research seminars in engineering systems, vol. 31,
pp. 1-9. Cambridge, MA, USA: MIT.

Cherry, K. 2020. "Kurt Lewin and Modern Social

Psychology." Verywell Mind. Retrieved from https://www.verywellmind.com/kurt-lewin-biography-1890-1947-2795540.

Coelho, E., & Basu, A. 2012. Effort estimation in agile software development using story points. *International Journal of Applied Information Systems* (IJAIS), 3(7).

Cohn, M. 2022. User stories. Mountain Goat Software. Retrieved from: https://www.mountaingoatsoftware.com/agile/user-stories.

Collins, J. C., & Porras, J. I. 1994. *Built to Last: Successful Habits of Visionary Companies*. New York, NY: Harper Business.

Collins, J. C. 2001. *Good to Great: Why Some Companies Make the Leap ... and Others Don't*. New York, NY: Harper Business.

Cottmeyer, M. E. 2011. "Large scale program and portfolio management with Scrum and Kanban." Paper presented at PMI® Global Congress 2011—North America, Dallas, TX. Newtown Square, PA: Project

Management Institute.

Corporate Finance Institute. 2022. "Strategic Planning." Retrieved from https://corporatefinanceinstitute.com/resources/knowledge/strategy/strategic-planning/.

cPrime. 2016. "Case study: Going agile on a grand scale." Retrieved from https://www.scrumalliance.org/ScrumRedesignDEVSite/media/ScrumAllianceMedia/Files%20and%20PDFs/Agile%20Resources/Sponsors/cPrime-CaseStudy-Agilent.pdf.

Crosby, P. 1979. *Quality is Free*. New York: McGraw-Hill.

Dam, R. F., & Siang, T. Y. 2022. "The history of design thinking." Retrieved from https://www.interaction-design.org/literature/article/design-thinking-get-a-quick-overview-of-the-history#:~:text=Cognitive%20scientist%20and%20Nobel%20Prize,as%20principles%20of%20design%20thinking.

Davis, T., & Higgins, J. 2013. "A Blockbuster Failure: How an Outdated Business Model Destroyed a Giant."

Chapter 11 *Bankruptcy Case Studies.*

Deming, W. E. 1986. *Out of Crisis.* Center for Advanced Engineering Study. Massachusetts Institute of Technology, Cambridge, MA.

Digital.AI. 2019. "13th Annual State of Agile Report." Retrieved from https://digital.ai/?s=13th+state+of+agile+report.

Dodd, V. 2021. "What is ISO 9001 & why is it Important?" Skillcast. Retrieved from https://www.skillcast.com/blog/why-iso-9001-is-important.

Dooley, B. 2023. "Toyota makes a change at the top as a Toyoda steps aside." The New York Times. January 26, 2023. Retrieved from https://www.nytimes.com/2023/01/26/business/toyota-ceo-toyoda.html.

Eden, C., and F. Ackermann. 1998. *Making Strategy: The Journey of Strategic Management.* Sage.

Emerson, M. S. 2022. "7 reasons why change management strategies fail and how to avoid them."

Harvard Professional Development. Retrieved from https://professional.dce.harvard.edu/blog/7-reasons-why-change-management-strategies-fail-and-how-to-avoid-them/#:~:text=However%2C%20change%20management%20strategies%20often,the%20organization%20or%20the%20team.

Everett, J. 2020. "What Is a Burn Up Chart?" Wrike. Retrieved from https://www.wrike.com/blog/what-is-a-burn-up-chart/.

Fayol, H. 1916. "General Principles of Management." *Classics of Organization Theory*, vol. 2, no. 15, 1916, pp. 57-69.

Fechter, J. 2021. "What Does a Product Owner Do? Roles and Responsibilities." Product Manager HQ. Retrieved from https://productmanagerhq.com/product-owner-job-description/.

Fourtané, S. 2020. "Sweden: How to Live in the World's First Cashless Society." Interesting Engineering. Retrieved from

https://interestingengineering.com/innovation/swede
n-how-to-live-in-the-worlds-first-cashless-society.

Fowler, M., and J. Highsmith. 2001. "The Agile Manifesto." *Software Development*, vol. 9, no. 8, 2001, pp. 28-35.

Gibbons, S. 2016. "Design Thinking 101." Nielsen Norman Group. Retrieved from https://www.nngroup.com/articles/design-thinking/.

Gimsley, S. 2022. "Systems Thinking in Management: Definition, Theory & Model." Study.com. Retrieved from https://study.com/learn/lesson/systems-thinking-approach-model.html.

Gleeson, L. 2018. "Organizational Change Can Really Hurt: 3 Ways to Manage Fear and Stay Energized." Forbes. March 23, 2018. Retrieved from https://www.forbes.com/sites/brentgleeson/2018/03/23/organizational-change-can-suck-3-ways-to-manage-fear-and-stay-energized/?sh=24effbe7609d.

Goncalves, L. 2020. "Agile Portfolio Management Definition and Principles." Adapt Methodology.

Retrieved from https://adaptmethodology.com/agile-portfolio-management/.

Goncalves, L. 2022. "Lean Change Management a Mandatory Approach for Every Executive Leader." Adapt Methodology. Retrieved from https://adaptmethodology.com/lean-change-management-model/.

Harrin, E. 2013. "What Goes in a Preliminary Program Business Case?" Projectmanagement.com. Retrieved from https://www.projectmanagement.com/blog-post/6715/what-goes-in-a-preliminary-program-business-case-.

Harrin, E. 2022. "5 Benefits of Program Management." Knowledge Hut. Retrieved from https://www.knowledgehut.com/blog/project-management/5-benefits-of-program-management.

Harisaiprasad, K. 2020. "COBIT 2019 and COBIT 5 Comparison." Retrieved from https://www.isaca.org/resources/news-and-trends/industry-news/2020/cobit-2019-and-cobit-5-

comparison.

Hatfield, C. 2016. "What Does a Program Manager Need to Execute on Strategy?" Retrieved from https://blog.planview.com/program-manager-strategy-execution/.

Heaslip, R. J. 2014. *Managing Complex Projects and Programs: How to Improve Leadership of Complex Initiatives Using a Third-Generation Approach.* Wiley.

Hook, C., Burge, R., and Bagg, J. 2017. "Routines for Results: A Quick-Reference Guidebook of End-to-End Solutions to Solidify Your Small Business." Productivity Press.

Invest Northern Ireland. 2023. "IT Risk Management." Retrieved from https://www.nibusinessinfo.co.uk/content/different-types-it-risk.

IT IP Law Group Europe. 2016. "Article 16: Right to Rectification." Retrieved from https://gdpr-expert.com/article.html?mid=6&id=16#textesofficiels .

IT IP Law Group Europe. 2016. "Article 5: Principles Relating to Processing of Personal Data." Retrieved from https://gdpr-expert.com/article.html?mid=6&id=5#textesofficiels.

ISACA CMMI Performance Solutions. 2022. "CMMI." Retrieved from https://cmmiinstitute.com/cmmi.

ISO. 2015. "Quality Management Principles." Retrieved from https://www.iso.org/publication/PUB100080.html.

ISO. 2022. "ISO 9000 Family." Retrieved from https://www.iso.org/iso-9001-quality-management.html#:~:text=In%20fact%2C%20there%20are%20over,process%20approach%20and%20continual%20improvement.

Jacob, J. 2021. "Why Projects Fail?" Retrieved from https://www.linkedin.com/pulse/why-projects-fail-msp-pmp-pmi-acp-csm-safe-5-agilist-itil-/.

Jenkins, J. G. 1940."Review of Management and the Worker: An Account of a Research Program Conducted by the Western Electric Company, Hawthorne Works, Chicago."

Johnson, S. 2019. "What Is the Meaning of Organizational Strategy?" Retrieved from https://smallbusiness.chron.com/meaning-organizational-strategy-59427.html.

Jones, G. R. 2013. *Organizational Theory, Design, and Change.* Upper Saddle River, NJ: Pearson.

Kaplan, R. & Norton, D. 1992. "The Balanced Scorecard: Measures That Drive Performance." *Harvard Business Review*, 70(1), 71-79.

Kaplan, R. & Norton, D. 2000. "Having Trouble with Your Strategy? Then Map It." *Harvard Business Review*. Retrieved from https://hbr.org/2000/09/having-trouble-with-your-strategy-then-map-it.

Kodwani, J. K. 2021. "All About PMI Agile Hybrid Project Pro Micro-Credential." Retrieved from https://medium.com/@jayant.kodwani/new-agile-hybrid-project-pro-micro-credential-from-pmi-coming-soon-in-april-2021-35dad3686039.

Kotter, J. 1995. "Leading Change: Why Transformation Efforts Fail." *Harvard Business Review*. Retrieved from https://hbr.org/1995/05/leading-change-why-transformation-efforts-fail-2.

Kotter, J. 2022. "Our Foundation: The 8 Steps for Leading Change." Retrieved from https://www.kotterinc.com/methodology/8-steps/.

Kübler-Ross Foundation. 2022. "Kübler-Ross Change Curve®." Retrieved from https://www.ekrfoundation.org/5-stages-of-grief/change-curve/.

Lai, E. 2022. "LACE & PMO – Do You Need Just One or Both?" Retrieved from https://www.cprime.com/resources/blog/lace-pmo-do-you-need-just-one-or-both/.

Lamorte, W. W. 2022. "Diffusion of Innovation Theory." Retrieved from https://sphweb.bumc.bu.edu/otlt/mph-modules/sb/behavioralchangetheories/behavioralchangetheories4.html.

LawInsider.com n.d. "Operations & Maintenance (O&M) Definition." Retrieved from https://www.lawinsider.com/dictionary/operations-maintenance-om.

Lavanya, N. & Malarvizhi, T. 2008. "Risk Analysis and Management: A Vital Key to Effective Project Management." Paper presented at PMI® Global Congress 2008—Asia Pacific, Sydney, New South Wales, Australia. Newtown Square, PA: Project Management Institute.

Lee, G. & Brumer, J. 2017. "Managing Mission-Critical Government Software Projects: Lessons Learned from Healthcare.gov Project." *The Business of Government*.

Leitner, P. M. 1999. "Japan's Post-War Economic Success: Deming, Quality, and Contextual Realities." *Journal of Management History*.

LeSS Company B.V. 2022. "Principles." Retrieved from https://less.works/less/principles.

Lewin, K. 1947. *Change Management Model*. New York, NY: McGraw Hill.

Lewin, K. 1951. *Field Theory in Social Science: Selected Theoretical Papers (Edited by Dorwin Cartwright.)*. Harpers.

Levinson, D. R. 2016. "HealthCare.gov: Case Study of CMS Management of the Federal Marketplace." U.S. Department of Health and Human Services Office of the Inspector General. Report #OEI-06-14-00350.

London, S. 2019. "How to Double the Odds That Your Change Program Will Succeed." Retrieved from https://www.mckinsey.com/capabilities/people-and-organizational-performance/our-insights/how-to-double-the-odds-that-your-change-program-will-succeed.

Mankins, M., Brahm, C., & Caimi, G. 2014. "Your Scarcest Resource." Harvard Business Review. Retrieved from https://hbr.org/2014/05/your-scarcest-resource.

Manzoor, Q. A. 2011. "Impact of Employees Motivation on Organizational Effectiveness." *European Journal of Business and Management*, 3(3), 36-44.

Mathenge, J., & Stevens-Hall, J. 2019. "The Seven ITIL 4 Guiding Principles." BMC Blogs. Retrieved from https://www.bmc.com/blogs/itil-guiding-principles/#:~:text=A%20guiding%20principle%20is

%20a,of%20work%2C%20or%20management%20structure.

Meadows, D. 2009. "Thinking in Systems: A Primer." London; Sterling, VA: Earthscan.

Mendelow, A. 1991. "Stakeholder mapping." In *Proceedings of the 2nd International Conference on Information Systems* (pp. 10-24).

Murray, B. 2023. "7 tips for running an impactful Scrum of Scrums." *Matrix Resources Blog*. Retrieved from https://www.matrixres.com/blog/2018/05/7-tips-for-running-an-impactful-scrum-of-scrums?source=google.com.

Murtell, J. 2021. "The 5 phases of design thinking." *AMA Marketing News*. Retrieved from https://www.ama.org/marketing-news/the-5-phases-of-design-thinking/#:~:text=The%20short%20form%20of%20the,%2C%20ideate%2C%20prototype%20and%20test.

Naybour, P. 2020." List and describe five benefits of programme management." *Parallel Project Training*

*Blog.* Retrieved from https://www.parallelprojecttraining.com/blog/list-and-describe-five-benefits-of-programme-management/.

O'Grady, J. 2021. "The Juran Trilogy." LibreTexts. Retrieved from https://bio.libretexts.org/Bookshelves/Biotechnology/Quality_Assurance_and_Regulatory_Affairs_for_the_Biosciences/02%3A_Introduction_to_Quality_Princ iples/2.03%3A_Section_3-.

Office of Government Commerce 2004. *Managing Successful Programmes.* Großbritannien. TSO.

On Strategy. 2018. "Who's responsible for what? Structuring your strategic plan." Retrieved from https://onstrategyhq.com/resources/whos-responsible-for-what-how-to-structure-your-strategic-plan/#:~:text=The%20CEO%20and%20executive%20team,achieve%20its%20vision%20of%20success .

Overeem, B. 2017. "The 8 stances of a scrum master." Retrieved from https://scrumorg-website-

prod.s3.amazonaws.com/drupal/2017-
05/The%208%20Stances%20of%20a%20Scrum%2
0Master%20Whitepaper%20v2_0.pdf.

Patanakul, P. 2008. "Program risk management: how it is done in major defense programs." Paper presented at PMI® Research Conference: *Defining the Future of Project Management*, Warsaw, Poland. Newtown Square, PA: Project Management Institute.

Peters, T. J., & Waterman, R. H. 1982. *In Search of Excellence: Lessons from America's Best-Run Companies.* New York: Harper & Row.

Peters, T. J. 1987. *Thriving on chaos.* New York: Random House.

Planview. 2021. "The state of strategy execution: Embracing uncertainty to adapt at speed." Retrieved from https://www.planview.com/lp/strategy-execution-benchmark-prm/.

Prasoon, A. 2020. "Develop a systems thinking mindset." Retrieved from https://www.linkedin.com/pulse/develop-systems-thinking-mindset-abhishek-prasoon-pmp-/.

Printz, L. 2023. "What Toyota's change in CEOs means for Its stock." Retrieved from https://www.fool.com/investing/2023/02/03/what-toyotas-change-in-ceos-means-for-its-stock/.

Product HQ. 2023. "What is the Large-Scale Scrum (LeSS) Framework?" Retrieved from https://producthq.org/agile/scrum/large-scale-scrum-less-framework/.

Project Management Institute. 2013. *A Guide to the Project Management Body of Knowledge.* Newtown Square, PA: Project Management Institute.

Project Management Institute. 2017. *The Standard for Program Management (4th ed.).* Newtown Square, PA: Project Management Institute.

Project Management Institute. 2021. *A Guide to the Project Management Body of Knowledge.* Newtown Square, PA: Project Management Institute.

Project Management Institute. 2023a. "Disciplined Agile® Delivery (DAD)." Retrieved from https://www.pmi.org/disciplined-agile/process/introduction-to-dad. Newtown Square,

PA: Project Management Institute.

Project Management Institute. 2023b. "Program Management." Retrieved from https://www.pmi.org/disciplined-agile/process/program-management. Newtown Square, PA: Project Management Institute.

Putre, L. 2016. "Building better supplier relationships at Ford." Retrieved from https://www.industryweek.com/manufacturing-leader-of-the-week/article/21971876/building-better-supplier-relationships-at-ford.

Radovanovic, D., Radojević, T., Lucic, D. & Šarac, M. 2010. "Audit in accordance with COBIT standard." 1137-1141. Retrieved from https://www.researchgate.net/figure/Standards-and-frameworks-that-are-used-for-planning-IT-audit-activity_fig4_224162993.

Ratnaraj, D. Y. 2014. "Agility with Quality — Discipline Delivers Excellence." Paper presented at PMI® Global Congress 2014—North America, Phoenix, AZ. Newtown Square, PA: Project Management

Institute.

Reich, B., and I. Benbaset. 2000. "Factors That Influence the Social Dimension of Alignment between Business and Information Technology Objectives." *MIS Quarterly* 24, no. 1 (2000): 81-113.

Reinhardt, A. 1998. "Steve Jobs: 'There's Sanity Returning'." Business Week, no. 25.

Roach, L. 2023. "Program Management: The Key to Strategic Execution." Retrieved from https://www.planview.com/resources/articles/program-management-key-strategic-execution/#:~:text=Program%20management%20enables%20the%20organization,knowledge%20about%20current%20organizational%20capabilities.

Royce, W. W. 1970. "Managing the development of large systems: Concepts and techniques." In *Proceedings of the 9th International Conference on Software Engineering* (pp. 328-38). ACM.

Scaled Agile Inc. 2023a. "Agile Release Train." Retrieved from https://www.scaledagileframework.com/agile-release-train/.

Scaled Agile Inc. 2023b. "SAFe Lean-Agile Principles." Retrieved from https://www.scaledagileframework.com/safe-lean-agile-principles/.

Scaled Agile Inc. 2023c. "Product Owner." Retrieved from https://www.scaledagileframework.com/product-owner/.

Scaled Agile Inc. 2023d. "Program Increment." Retrieved from https://www.scaledagileframework.com/program-increment/.

Scaled Agile Inc. 2023e. "Release Train Engineer." Retrieved from https://www.scaledagileframework.com/release-train-engineer/.

Schuurman, R. 2020. "Product owner vs product manager." Retrieved from https://medium.com/the-value-maximizers/product-owner-vs-product-manager-67cf60575f98.

Schwaber, K., & Sutherland, J. 2011. "The Scrum Guide." Scrum Alliance, 21(19), 1.

Schwaber, K., & Sutherland, J. 2020. "The Scrum Guide." Retrieved from https://scrumguides.org/docs/scrumguide/v2020/2020-Scrum-Guide-US.pdf#zoom=100.

Scrum Alliance Inc. 2022. "Scrum Principles." Retrieved from https://www.scrumalliance.org/about-scrum#!section4.

Scott, L. 2016. "Baldridge Key Terms: Strategic Objectives." Retrieved from https://www.nist.gov/baldrige/self-assessing/baldrige-key-terms.

Seaman, C., & Guo, Y. 2011. "Measuring and monitoring technical debt." In *Advances in Computers* (Vol. 82, pp. 25-46). Elsevier.

Shaban, H. 2022. "5 types of organizational change and how to manage them." Retrieved from https://www.apty.io/blog/types-of-organizational-change.

Shafayet, F. 2022. "How to improve product adoption with customer success." Retrieved from https://www.timetackle.com/how-to-improve-product-adoption-with-customer-success/.

Shepard, G. 2022. "It's never too early to establish your company's North Star." Retrieved from https://chiefexecutive.net/never-establish-company-north-star/.

St Clair, R. 2022. "Who needs ISO certification? 7 industries in need of ISO 9001 certification." Retrieved from https://www.qms.com.au/blog-post/7-industries-in-need-of-iso-9001-certification/.

Stewart, J. 2022. "Top 10 reasons why projects fail." Retrieved from https://project-management.com/top-10-reasons-why-projects-fail/.

Stobierski, T. 2020. "Organizational change management: what it is & why it's important." Retrieved from: https://online.hbs.edu/blog/post/organizational-change-management#:~:text=Why%20Is%20Organizational%20Change%20Management,and%20work%20effectively%20during%20it.

Stobierski, T. 2021. "Resource management plan: what it is & how to create one." Retrieved from

https://www.northeastern.edu/graduate/blog/resourc
e-management-plan/.

Suarez, J. G. 1992. "Three experts on Quality
Management: Philip B. Crosby, W. Edwards
Deming, Joseph M. Juran." Total Quality Leadership
Office, Arlington VA.

Sutherland, J. 2001. "Agile can scale: Inventing and
reinventing SCRUM in five companies." *Cutter IT
Journal*, 14(21), 5-11.

Sveriges Riksbank. 2020. "Payments in Sweden 2020."
Retrieved from https://www.riksbank.se/en-
gb/payments--cash/payments-in-sweden/payments-
in-sweden-2020/1.-the-payment-market-is-being-
digitalised/why-are-people-in-sweden-no-longer-
using-cash/.

Swedish Institute. 2021. "A cashless society." Retrieved
from https://sweden.se/life/society/a-cashless-
society.

SweetProcess. 2019. "The definitive guide to
organizational change management." Retrieved
from https://www.sweetprocess.com/organizational-

change-management/.

Tableau Software, LLC. 2022. "A guide to data driven decision making: What it is, its importance, & how to implement it." Retrieved from https://www.tableau.com/learn/articles/data-driven-decision-making#:~:text=What%20is%20data%2Ddriven%20decision,goals%2C%20objectives%2C%20and%20initiatives.

Tallon, P. P., & Pinsonneault, A. 2011. "Competing perspectives on the link between strategic information technology alignment and organizational agility: Insights from a mediation model." *MIS Quarterly*, 35(2), 463-486.

Taylor, F. W. 1919. *The Principles of Scientific Management*. New York: Harper & Brothers.

Technopedia.com. 2017. "Software development." Retrieved from https://www.techopedia.com/definition/16431/software-development.

TechTarget. 2023. "Kanban." Retrieved from

https://www.techtarget.com/whatis/definition/kanban
.

Thiry, M. 2015. *Program Management.* Ashgate Publishing Ltd.

Thomas, M. 2019. "COBIT 2019 governance and management objectives guidance." Retrieved from https://www.youtube.com/watch?v=zMUVjQvJXwU.

Thompson, K. 2013. "Recipes for Agile Governance in the Enterprise (RAGE)." Retrieved from https://www.cprime.com/wp-content/uploads/woocommerce_uploads/2013/07/RAGE-Final-cPrime1.pdf.

Tkachuk, K. 2021. "What is technical debt and how to tackle it?" Retrieved from https://www.edvantis.com/blog/technical-debt/#what-is-technical-debt.

ToolsQA. 2021. "Waterfall method." Retrieved from https://www.toolsqa.com/software-testing/waterfall-model/.

Townsend, S. 2022. "Top 12 resource management best

practices." Retrieved from https://www.planview.com/resources/guide/resource -management-software/top-12-resource- management-best-practices/.

Tuckman, B. W. 1965. "Developmental sequence in small groups." *Psychological Bulletin*, 63(6), 384-399.

U.S. Department of Health & Human Services. 2022. "HIPAA for professionals." Retrieved from https://www.hhs.gov/hipaa/for- professionals/index.html.

U.S. Environmental Protection Agency. 2021. "Lean thinking and methods – Kaizen." Retrieved from https://www.epa.gov/sustainability/lean-thinking- and-methods- kaizen#:~:text=Kaizen%2C%20or%20rapid%20impr ovement%20processes,and%20processes%20of%2 0an%20organization.

Vejseli, S., Rossmann, A., & Garidis, K. 2022. "The concept of agility in IT governance and its impact on firm performance." Retrieved from https://www.researchgate.net/profile/Konstantin-

Garidis/publication/362326327_The_Concept_of_A gility_in_IT_Governance_and_its_Impact_on_Firm_ Performance/links/62e3a1187782323cf1832b41/Th e-Concept-of-Agility-in-IT-Governance-and-its-Impact-on-Firm-Performance.pdf.

Viter, I. 2022. "How to Do Resource Forecasting - A Complete Guide." Retrieved from https://www.runn.io/blog/resource-forecasting#:~:text=Resource%20forecasting%20is %20a%20method,which%20they%20will%20be%20 needed.

VMWare. 2022. "What Is DevSecOps?" Retrieved from https://www.vmware.com/topics/glossary/content/de vsecops.html.

Von Bertalanffy, L. 1950. "An Outline of General System Theory." *British Journal for the Philosophy of Science.*

WalkMe Team. 2021. "5 Types of Organizational Change." Retrieved from https://change.walkme.com/5-types-of-organizational-change/.

Waterman, R. H., and T. J. Peters. 1982. *In Search of*

*Excellence: Lessons from America's Best-Run Companies.* New York: Harper & Row.

Waters, S. 2022. "Why Building Great Work Relationships Is More Than Just Getting Along." Retrieved from https://www.betterup.com/blog/building-good-work-relationships.

Weber, M. 1978. *Economy and Society: An Outline of Interpretive Sociology*, edited by G. Roth and C. Wittich. Berkley, California: University of California Press.

Wendler, R. 2013. "The Structure and Components of Agility–A Multi-Perspective View." *Informatyka Ekonomiczna* 28: 148-169.

Worley, Christopher G., Thomas D. Williams, and Edward E. Lawler III. 2014. *The Agility Factor: Building Adaptable Organizations for Superior Performance.* John Wiley & Sons.

Worley, Christopher G., Thomas D. Williams, and Edward E. Lawler III. 2014. *Assessing Organization Agility: Creating Diagnostic Profiles to Guide Transformation.* John Wiley & Sons.

Work Institute. 2020. "2020 Retention Report." Retrieved from https://info.workinstitute.com/hubfs/2020%20Retention%20Report/Work%20Institutes%202020%20Retention%20Report.pdf.

Yauch, Charles A. 2011. "Measuring Agility as a Performance Outcome." *Journal of Manufacturing Technology Management*.

Yusuf, Yahya Y., M. Sarhadi, and A. Gunasekaran. 1999. "Agile Manufacturing: The Drivers, Concepts, and Attributes." *International Journal of Production Economics* 62 (1-2): 33-43.

Zax, David. 2011. "Dish Buys Blockbuster for $320 Million. Why?" Retrieved from https://www.fastcompany.com/1745065/dish-buys-blockbuster-320-million-why.

Zein, Ofer. 2010. "Roles, Responsibilities, and Skills in Program Management." Paper presented at *PMI®️ Global Congress 2010*—EMEA, Milan, Italy. Newtown Square, PA: Project Management Institute.

# Appendix E: Index of Key Terms

# Appendix E:
# Index of Key Concepts and Terms

# About the Author

Jim Carilli, PhD, MBA, PfMP, PgMP, PMP, CSM, ITIL-F, SAFe® SA/LPM, AWS-CCP

Over his 30-year career in project, program, and portfolio management, Jim Carilli has had the pleasure of working with teams in a variety of organizations, allowing him to hone his skills and develop fresh ideas about the way that organizations can run more efficiently and effectively, leading teams to create a productive environment with a positive work culture. Jim has led teams at Aetna, KPMG, Deloitte, Computer Sciences Corporation, and PricewaterhouseCoopers, among others.

Currently, he is an associate partner/senior program manager at IBM.

This book was inspired not only by his career in project and program management but also by his work outside the office in developing literature on management, including the research he performed for his doctoral dissertation, "The perceived effectiveness of the Scaled Agile Framework® in software development organizations: A mixed methods exploratory case study."

Jim's expertise in the management arena has been utilized in his role as a subject matter expert reviewer for two of PMI's ANSI-accredited peer-reviewed foundational standards, including *The Standard for Program Management*, fourth edition, PMI (2017), and A Guide to the Project Management Body of Knowledge (*PMBOK Guide*), sixth edition (2017). Jim helped lead the development of the first edition of PMI's *Requirements Management: A Practice Guide* (2016) as the vice chairperson and a contributing author. Earlier, in 2013, Jim served as a core team member and contributing author for a significant update to the third edition of *The Standard for Program Management*. He also served as a reviewer for

*The PMBOK Guide*, fifth edition (2013), and *The Standard for Portfolio Management*, third edition, PMI (2012).

Jim has been a contributing author for multiple peer-reviewed publications, including those published by the Academy of Human Resource Development, Scrum Alliance, and Project Management Institute's Annual Global Congress. As a guest lecturer at the American University, Kogod School of Management, Jim has addressed MBA students on program management, project management, and agile methods and practices.

A retired Army Medical Service Corps officer for the U.S. Army National Guard, Jim holds a Ph.D. in technology management from Indiana State University, an M.B.A. from Virginia Polytechnic Institute and State University, and a B.S. in management information systems from Central Connecticut State University.

Jim also holds a variety of certifications, including the Portfolio Management Professional (PfMP), Program Management Professional (PgMP), and Project Management Professional (PMP) from the Project Management Institute; Agile certifications, including Certified Scrum Master (CSM) from the Scrum Alliance;

and Scaled Agilist (SA) and Lean Portfolio Manager (LPM) certifications from Scaled Agile, Inc. He also holds several technical certifications including the Information Technology Infrastructure Library Foundation certificate in Service Management, and several certifications and badges provided by Atlassian, AWS, PwC, and IBM.

Jim resides in Florida with his wife Debi and three dogs who focus on a different type of agility.

Connect with Jim at www.ProgramAgility.com.

www.ingramcontent.com/pod-product-compliance
Lightning Source LLC
Chambersburg PA
CBHW071536210326
41597CB00019B/3025